SQUIRREL CAGE JAIL

Council Bluffs, Iowa

S. M. SENDEN

Palmetto Publishing Group
Charleston, SC

Squirrel Cage Jail

First Edition

Printed in the United States

ISBN-13: 978-1-64111-303-8
ISBN-10: 1-64111-303-0

DEDICATION

This book is dedicated to special deputy Claude B. Dail who lost his life at the Pottawattamie County Jail when a riot gun accidently discharged during the Farmer's Holiday Rebellion in 1932.

TABLE OF CONTENTS

PREFACE

To say the least, the Squirrel Cage Jail is a unique and fascinating architectural structure in the history of penal institutions. To some, the concept of a rotary jail defies description where only seeing is truly understanding. I hope that these pages will begin to reveal more to those who have not yet had the chance to see the jail for themselves; and, for those who have been to the Squirrel Cage Jail, this book will enrich their visit and entice others to experience it for themselves.

For some, any jail is a completely alien institution that has never touched the perimeter of their lives. For others, it is a part of their life and culture. No matter where you locate yourself in the spectrum of experiences of the penal system, you will, undoubtedly find this to be one of the most unusual institutions ever conceived of in prison history. I have enjoyed getting to know more about the jail, becoming familiar with the layout, artifacts, stories and staff. I have had the privilege to meet people who have returned to the jail to see it once again, since the time they spent a few nights locked up in one of the cells within the rotary section of the jail. Some have said the experience was so horrendous that they would exchange a longer time served in any other prison than come again to the Squirrel Cage Jail.

The Squirrel Cage, rear elevation, was built in 1885. Within the walls are located the bullpen and rotary device that makes this building unique. The warden's apartment was on the top floor.

Those of us who relate history spend many hours in painstaking research, reading and rereading old documents, publications, diaries and newspaper articles. We even conduct interviews with people who recollect some nugget of the past in relation to the subject of our research. All too often we find that the old accounts do not always agree with one another, memories fade and sometimes distort events of the past, at times conflating their recollections with other memories or events. Yet nonetheless, history and the past are alluring, drawing us in to another place and time.

The past captures our imagination; it gets under our skin. It haunts our dreams as we begin to open the doors of history in dusty old record rooms, photos and writings of those who went before us. The oral history related to us draws us in as memories of another time cloud the room, thick with the dusty cobwebs of time. As a historian I attempt as best I can to unravel the tangled skein of threads of the past and hopefully weave them into a tapestry that gives a coherent picture of events that invites the reader to enter this world, and bring to mind their own memories and experiences, so that they may relate the stories again to another generation keeping the history alive.

The idea for this book arose out of an article Sergeant Jason LeMaster of the Pottawattamie County Sheriff's Police wrote back in 2014. This article captured my imagination and invited me to get to know more about the Squirrel Cage Jail and ultimately to write this book. Sergeant LeMaster's article began with these sentences: *It all started with a small newspaper clipping. Yellowed with age and somehow, remarkably, not lost in the hustle and bustle of life. This small article written in 1932 provided a window to the past and the history of the Squirrel Cage Jail in Council Bluffs, Iowa, and a part of history that should have been honored.*

LeMaster reveals his own curiosity and growing interest in what happened in 1932.

Early in 2013, while speaking with Ed Ritchie & Carla Borgaila with the Historical Society of Pottawattamie County, I was asked if I had ever heard of a Deputy being shot and killed inside the Squirrel Cage Jail. As far as I knew, the Pottawattamie County Sheriff's Office has only recorded two deaths. In 1911, Deputy Clarence Woolman was shot and killed by Dr. H. D. Kelly while transporting the prisoner to the Inobriate Hospital in Knoxville, Iowa. Dr. Kelly was found not guilty by reason of insanity and sent to a mental hospital. On January 9, 1915, he was declared sane and released. In 1981, Chief Deputy Duane Otto was fatally injured when a roof of a porch fell on him as deputies were entering a home of a man who was threatening to kill his wife and threatening suicide.

So, of course this information was new to me and to the Sheriff's Office. I was then able to get a copy of this newspaper article and start researching anything and everything that I could find. Since the original article was from 1932, my research capabilities were limited. However, what I was able to find was remarkable. I learned all about The Farmer's Holiday Strike. I also learned that with the increase threat of violence in the area that Sheriff Lainson needed good brave men. As new Deputies were being sworn in to serve the citizens of Pottawattamie County, he also swore in several Special Deputies to help guard against any revolt against the jail. In Council Bluffs in 1932 there was no shortage of good brave men. Sheriff Lainson found several citizens who were veterans of the war that were well trained, and willing to stand on the side of the law.

As an apologia, please forgive any errors on my relating of what I have discovered. As with any history there is always contradictory information; dates, spelling of names and places and relating of the facts. I invite anyone with stories, artifacts or memories of the Squirrel Cage Jail to share them with the staff, so that your particular piece of this history will be recorded and not lost to time. Each story, incident, event and artifact only enrich the history of the jail for future generations.

Upon entering the jail the steel stairway leads to the upper floors.

As with any book there are many people who have helped make it a reality. No author works completely alone, especially on a book like this. Special thanks to Kat Slaughter for her endless patience in answering my questions, speedy assistance to my needs for access to the building, and especially, her gentle care of the jail itself. Thanks also to Jason LeMaster for his assistance. Not only did he peak my interest with his articles about Officer Dail, but with the history of the jail itself. To Jon Barnes, Trudy Beno, and the members of the board who each have a passion about the jail, history and Council Bluffs. Also, thanks to P. G. Roeder for proofreading, and Barbara Clarke for running a few facts to ground for me.

If you are able to, I would urge you to spend some time at the Squirrel Cage Jail where you may find yourself completely captivated and enamored by the unusual and incredible design of the structure. But be careful, you may get lost in the whispers of time that bring the past to life again as your fingers brush up against the peeling gray paint on the walls. If, in your time there, don't be too alarmed if you see something, a shadow of movement from the corner of your eye, that turning to look eludes your sight. Or maybe the sound of someone walking the empty corridor, or the impish laughter of the girls playing on the 4th floor. Take in a deep breath and the fragrances of the past may wash over you, some not so sweetly pleasant. For those who are fortunate enough, you may even encounter some of the many ghostly spirits that still inhabit the jail.

Please note that the photographs in this volume are used with permission and are primarily from the collection of the Squirrel Cage Jail, the Council Bluffs Public Library, Sergeant Jason LeMaster and the private collection of the author. Other images used are credited to the photographer.

NEED FOR A JAIL

How the idea was conceived to build a rotary jail is lost to time. Circular prisons had been in use since the 1790's though they were stationary with cells in the outside walls. The panopticon prison in England was built in 1791, from a design by English philosopher and social theorist, Jeremy Bentham. In 1800 Benjamin Latrobe built a variation of Bentham's panopticon prison to serve as the State Prison in Richmond, Virginia. In 1826 the Western Penitentiary in Pittsburg, Pennsylvania utilized the panopticon design, while in 1919 the State Prison in Statesville, Illinois was built utilizing four circular buildings. These round jails preserve an era, a movement and a reaction to the events of the time, as a radically new idea in incarceration took hold in the Midwest.

Two men from Indianapolis, Indiana, William Brown and B. F. H. Hough, patented and sold the idea of this unique rotary jail across the Midwest in the early 1880's. The Patent number 244,358 filed in the United States Patent Office 12 July of 1881 stated:

> *The object of our invention is to produce a jail or prison in which prisoners can be controlled without the necessity of personal contact between them and the jailer or guard, and incidentally to provide it with sundry conveniences and advantages not usually found in prisons. Attention is called to the fact, in this connection, that the construction of the cells is such that the prisoners cannot communicate with each other in any way, and therefore that any concert of action between them would be extremely difficult. The prisoners are handled without any possible chance of personal contact with*

any except the one desired, as the cell structure is rotated until the door opening of the cell desired is brought opposite the general door-opening in the outside grating, and while one cell occupies this position the rest must of necessity be securely closed. This arrangement makes the whole prison as convenient to the keeper as though it consisted of but a single prisoner.

These documents also contained detailed explanations of the jail and some illustrations. The essential core of the jail that was to be used as the detention facility, consisted of a three-story metal drum measuring twenty-eight feet high and twenty-four feet in diameter. The cells on the drum were divided into pie shaped cells with ten per level and two men to a cell. This drum revolved within a fixed metal cage with bars that were described as "heavier than those used to contain African lions." There was only one opening on each level so that entrance to each cell was gained when the cylinder, or rotating drum, was rotated to a fixed position where a cell doorway lined up with the outer cage opening.

The Montgomery County rotary jail in Crawfordsville, Indiana was built in 1881. The two-story jail served as the county jail until 1973. The Thirty-two-ton rotary mechanism was immobilized in the 1930's. In 1975, when the jail became preserved as a museum, the rotary mechanism was restored to working condition as it was designed and one person, by the turn of the hand crank, is able to rotate the entire jail drum once again.

These rotary jails were exclusively located in the central part of the nation. No records remain of how many of these structures were built, but at least five more rotary jails were built in the Midwest in the 1880's. The DeKalb County Jail located in Maryville, Missouri was built 1885, then dismantled 1938 when the county built a new courthouse and jail. The Daviess County Jail in Gallatin, Missouri was built in 1888. The Montgomery County Jail located in Crawfordsville, Indiana was built in 1882. The Sedgwick County Jail in Wichita, Kansas was built about 1884 or 1885 and due to popular complaint, this jail was dismantled in 1919 or 1920. The Pottawattamie County Jail of Council Bluffs, Iowa was built in 1885 and decommissioned in 1969. Only three of these exceptional structures remain, the rest have gone the way of the wrecking ball.

The rotary jail in Gallatin, Missouri survives as the only single-story rotary jail in the nation.

Rotary jails were most commonly built with a one- or two-story design. Only one three-story rotary jail was erected, and this was the one in

Council Bluffs, Iowa. The basic design of the jail hardly varied from the one- to the three-story structure. Preserved in the Nodaway County Jail in Maryville, Missouri which was a two-tier structure with little variation from the three-story jail in Pottawattamie County, the names of the patentees and designers are visible on the metal plate on the huge drum: W H Brown, patentee, and Haugh, Ketcham Co. designers, both of Indianapolis, Indiana.

EARLY DAYS

In 1804 President Thomas Jefferson bought a great swath of land from France consisting of 530 million acres. This great expanse of land needed to be explored. President Jefferson commissioned Meriwether Lewis and William Clark to explore those lands of the Louisiana Purchase. On August 4, 1804 Lewis and Clark recorded in their journal for their Corps of Discovery Expedition a meeting with the Oto and Missouri Nations at the foot of a high promontory along the banks of the Missouri River. The designation of this area became known as the Council Bluff a name which was adopted by trappers, traders and river navigators to describe the area on both sides of the Missouri River.

In 1837, soon after the Blackhawk Wars, the Native Americans of the Pottawattamie, Ottawa and Chippewa Nations settled in the area that we know today as Council Bluffs. They peacefully relocated from Chicago under the guidance of Billy Caldwell, called Chief Sauganash. In 1846 they were relocated to the Kansas Territory under a new treaty. Within two years of the 1844 death of the Mormon leader Joseph Smith at the hands of violent mobs in Nauvoo, Illinois, the Apostle Orson Hyde led a group of fellow Mormons to the abandoned settlement along the Missouri River. The Mormons took up residence creating a peaceful town they named Kanesville.

Between 1849 to 1851 the little settlement of Kanesville, that was renamed Council Bluffs, grew quickly. The discovery of gold at Sutter's Mill in California transformed the area as it became one of the major gateways to the west along the Mormon Trail. George Simons drawings illustrate the burgeoning town. The influx of gold seekers created the need for a Courthouse and the Cottonwood Jail.

Discovery of gold at Sutter's Mill in California in 1849 brought sweeping changes across the nation and had massive repercussions on the little settlement then known as Kanesville, Iowa. Gold fever inflamed the nation, and by 1850 a steady stream of humanity passed through Council Bluffs on their way west, seeking their dreams of golden riches and utilizing the Mormon Trail as one of the major highways that wound its way to the west. Many of those seeking to make their fortune in the gold fields flooded through the Council Bluffs area.

The influx of gold-seekers changed Kanesville irrevocably. Flagrant gambling cropped up on sidewalks and the liquor trade flourished. All manner of low-life speculators, gamblers and opportunists, men seeking an easy buck, men of the worst sort of every base calling and persuasion flooded the area. Along with the flood of unsavory men also came the camp followers, the women of ill-fame, plying their trade. These men lived hard, played hard, drank excessively and whored with the available soiled doves of easy virtue who had washed up on the shores of the Missouri River.

In the spring of 1848 Brigham Young led four thousand of the faithful to the Great Salt Lake. Other Mormons remained, making Kanesville/Council Bluffs the main outfitting post for travelers coming west. Long lines of migrant groups wound their way along the Mormon Trail. In 1852 Brigham Young sent instructions for the faithful to come to Utah. Some 2,500 Mormons set out on the long trek, carrying all they could in hand carts. Once again, the settlement was nearly deserted. With the Mormon exodus the population had dwindled to eight or nine hundred people. An outbreak of cholera drastically reduced the remaining population.

Once the Mormon control of the area slipped away, combined with the influx of gold-seekers passing through town, the need to establish a system of courts, a jail and a method of policing became necessary. In the early days, they had only one marshal, no courthouse, nor any jail. Much of city business was conducted in log meeting rooms like Beebee Hall or in other log shacks until someplace suitable could be procured.

Dexter Bloomer, an early resident of Council Bluffs, commented that every available building had been converted into a gambling den or drinking hall. The need for law and order grew as the population swelled. As the city established a government, the necessity grew for dedicated county and city buildings. For many years the district court was held in rented rooms in the City Hotel.

The need for a jail prompted swift action coming hard upon the heels of securing the courthouse. A calaboose committee was formed, and in 1849, the committee recommended the procurement of a house suitable to convert to a jail. They opted for a log house owned by Alderman Jonathan Stutsman, though the building needed repairs. Stutsman offered it to the county free for a year. They relocated the building in 1849 to Vine and Market Streets. Repairs were made under the watchful eye of Judge Frank Street. Three-inch nails were pounded into the planking and doubled over to cover the cottonwood joints of the log structure. More nails were driven into the logs to prevent prisoners from sawing their way out of the jail. The old accounts of its dimensions do not agree. Some relate that the Cottonwood Jail was twelve feet square, others claim it was fourteen feet square, and yet another account relates the building was eighteen feet square. It was furnished with a bunk, table and two chairs as well as a woodburning stove.

A log cabin was purchased and refitted to become what was called the Cottonwood Jail. Cottonwood weatherboards were nailed to the exterior of the cabin, doubling the thickness with the hopes of preventing prisoners from escaping.

Quite soon it became evident that the Cottonwood Jail was too small and antiquated to serve the growing problems in crime that plagued Pottawattamie County. In 1862 the Cottonwood Jail was sold to the city of Council Bluffs for $100. Previously prisoners had been housed in hotels around town. In January 1855, a prisoner housed at the Pacific House managed to escape. Sadly, on November 29, 1866, the Cottonwood Jail caught fire with a prisoner inside. It was suspected that he was attempting to burn the building down in the hope of escape.

The county built a new brick courthouse, as the old log courthouse had been outgrown. Officials placed the jail in the basement of the courthouse. The new jail proved to be no deterrent for escaping prisoners. More than once prisoners burrowed their way out of the basement. One man successfully dug his way out of the jail using a poker. In 1879 police arrested a group of tramps and locked them in the jail. Twenty men were placed within a ten-foot by fourteen-foot sized cell. The next morning, when police came to bring the men to court, only a few remained. The men had burrowed through the foundation leaving a large gaping hole in the stone and brickwork. Though patched later that day, the foundations had been seriously compromised. The courthouse stood for seventeen years before it was deemed unsafe and condemned, greatly due to the failing foundation walls. This left Pottawattamie County in need of a stronger jail that would be more difficult from which to escape.

The old log courthouse no longer could accommodate the needs of the growing city and county. The Cottonwood Jail had been sold to the city but had burned down taking the life of one prisoner. In 1866 lots were purchased at Pearl and 5th Street to build a brick courthouse that would have a jail in the basement level. Over the seventeen years the courthouse was in use, prisoners had burrowed their way out of the brick basement sometimes using a poker to cut through the brick. No matter how often the damage was repaired, ultimately, the foundations were weakened to a point that caused the building to be condemned.

The decade of 1860-1870 proved to be wrought with mob violence in several areas in Iowa. Some sixty men were lynched for violent crimes. The population in Council Bluffs nearly tripled bringing an increase in murders, arson, and other violent crimes that were unheard of when the Mormons were the primary residents. Crime across the State of Iowa and neighboring states was on the rise. The rise in crime was also attributable to the depression, which came from the post-Civil War economy; in response, the State Legislature reinstated capital punishment.

Confederate guerrilla and outlaw gangs, including that of Jesse James, terrorized Iowa, Missouri and even spread their terror into Minnesota. These were the sort of criminals that cities in the Midwest needed to confine. Jails of the past were not suitable for the new generation of criminals.

Desperately looking for a 'proper' jail, the Pottawattamie County Board of Supervisors researched their options. According to their minutes, as early as June 9, 1882, the County Board of Supervisors was inspecting a set of plans from Eckel and Mann Company for a revolutionary new concept in prisons: the rotary jail. In this 1882 meeting the County Board of Supervisors minutes read that the jail was "said to be agreeable to the Board in every respect. Said jail to have acomadions [sic] for eighty prisoners. Said jail to be built after the Patent of Haugh, Ketcham and Company known as the rotary jail . . . Said jail to be in no wise inferior to the jail and sheriff's residence built in Crawfordsville, Indiana by Haugh, Ketcham Company."

In February 1884 the Board met with the architect from Eckel and Mann Company and with delegates from various townships to take action for building a new jail. The County Board of Supervisors accepted the plans, stating that they were the best option best adapted for the county's use. The same firm had already built the rotary jail for Nodaway County in Maryville, Missouri. Possible factors in convincing the board to opt for the rotary jail plan was the cost of the building, savings in manpower and salaries, as well as the recent construction of the rotary jail in Maryville.

One of the main selling points for this unique style of prison was that one man could turn the entire cell drum using a large hand crank. The crank was accessible at any of the three levels and a security door was in place at the other levels when access to the desired cell was needed. The entire cell unit was one unit, thus when the cells were rotated to the opening three of the cells were aligned with the door, one per level.

In February of 1884 the Pottawattamie County Board of Supervisors agreed to build the rotary jail, keeping in mind the factors of cost to construct, maintain and man.

There were those who were not convinced that this new sort of jail was a good investment. Some made fun of the revolutionary design. Some accused the County Board of Supervisors of being too cheap to build a conventional jail. Jokes of the day labeled it *Hotel de Guittar*, so named for the then current sheriff Theodore Guittar who must have been in favor of the rotary jail.

Construction moved ahead rapidly. The jail was built with brick, steel and iron plating. Most of the required iron plating and steel were manufactured by the Haugh Ketcham Company of Indianapolis, Indiana, saving the builders time and money to get them custom-made to specifications. According to an article in the *Globe*, the cost to build the jail was $7,350 for the building and another $21,000 for the steel and iron work. Compared to other building options of the day this was a vast savings for the county. With great ceremony, on September 10, 1885 fifteen prisoners were transferred from the old courthouse jail to the new rotary jail.

Designs for a new jail were sought by the County Board of Supervisors. In 1884 the Board voted to build a revolutionary, new design in penal architecture. One of the selling points being that it would cost under $30,000 and would need less manpower to operate the facility.

INVENTION AND PATENT

If one tries to describe the Squirrel Cage Jail to someone who has never seen it, words fail to completely convey a clear image of how the jail looked and worked, for it is truly unique in the history of penal architecture.

The exterior of the jail was not designed to mimic contemporary penal institutions of the era that were built like fortresses. The jail resembles a brick Victorian carriage house standing three stories tall.

Construction moved quickly, and the result was a jail that looked more like a large Victorian carriage house than a jail. Some people laughed at this style of jail and called it *Hotel de Guittar*, so named for the Sheriff Theodore Guittar.

The front third of the building was dedicated to the housing of the jailer, with family's quarters that had high arched windows on the majority of the fourth floor. There were also some small rooms for storage and mechanical parts for supporting the rotary structure in the center. This also provided ventilation and access to the latrine system for maintenance and repairs. The kitchen was located on the ground floor across from the warden's offices. It was used for cooking the meals for the prisoners. When the building was built in 1885 there was no central heating or air-conditioning in any part of the building. The only source for warmth was the coal burning stove in the kitchen. The back section of the jail was dedicated to the rotary cells for minor offenders, the rotary mechanism, and prisoner exercise areas or common room. A later addition installed in the 1930's in this area was the shower, when running water was piped into this section of the building.

The front part of the second floor above the warden's offices consisted of individual cells for the women prisoners, and juveniles. At some point around 1960 the section of cells above the kitchen was converted to a bedroom and bath for the jailer and his wife. The back section of the jail cells was where offenders with a greater level of criminal offence were housed.

The third-floor front area contained the infirmary and room for those prisoners who had earned the designation of trusty. The jail cells on this level in the rotary section of the jail were dedicated to the worst, most violent of the offenders housed in the jail.

The jail itself consists of a large room 36 feet by 36 feet and 28 feet high in the rear of the building that still houses the rotary unit and the cage. This is a large gridded, stationary, cylindrical cage bolted to the floor and also to the iron plates in the ceiling.

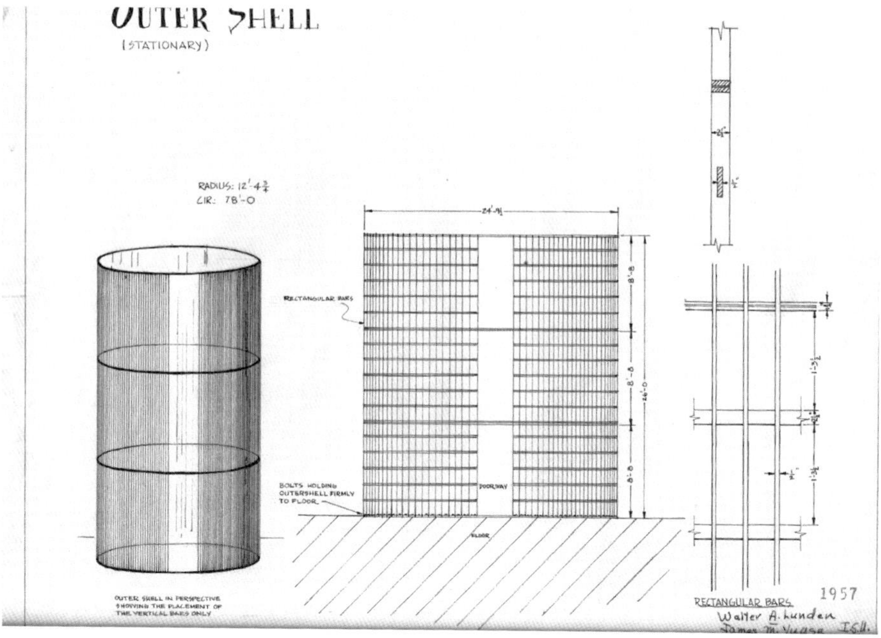

The original blueprints for the building have been lost. In 1957 Walter Lunden and James Yuasa of Iowa State University attempted to recreate the blueprints for the Pottawattamie County Jail. Their detailed drawings give the dimensions of the outer shell of the cage.

Inside this gridded drum is the inner rotary cylinder divided into three levels or decks, each segmented into ten pie-shaped cells. The inner cylinder is constructed around a central axis which rests on bearings at the base, with a supporting collar on the third floor.

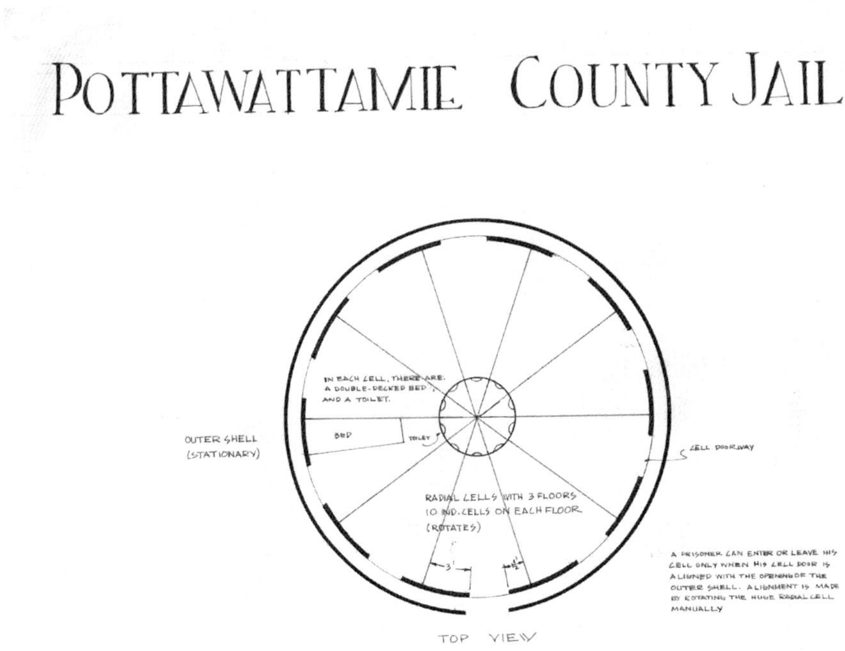

The design displays a top view of the cage and rotary cell structure illustrating the cell dimensions, the entry to each cell, where the cots were affixed to the walls, and the location of the toilets.

The design of the jail allowed limited access to the cells. There is one door at each level in the outer cage. Each cell in the inner drum has a doorway, but no door. Entrance is gained to a cell by rotating the inner cylinder to align with the outer stationary cylinder.

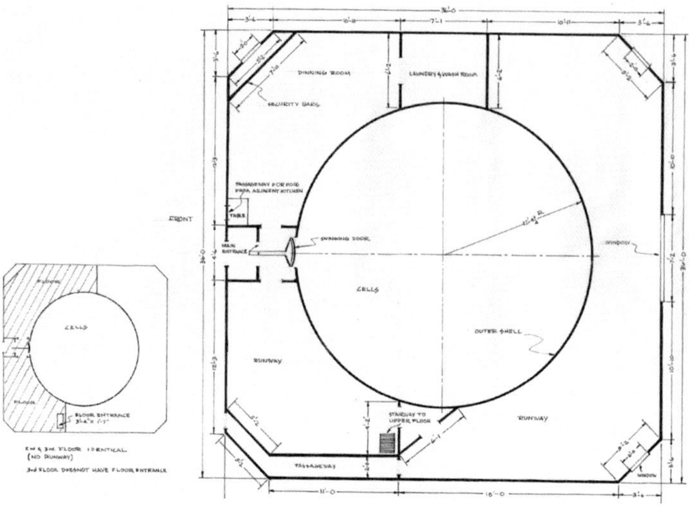

Plans lay out the basic floorplan for each level of the three-tiered rotary jail with explanation of differences from the ground floor and the second and third tier.

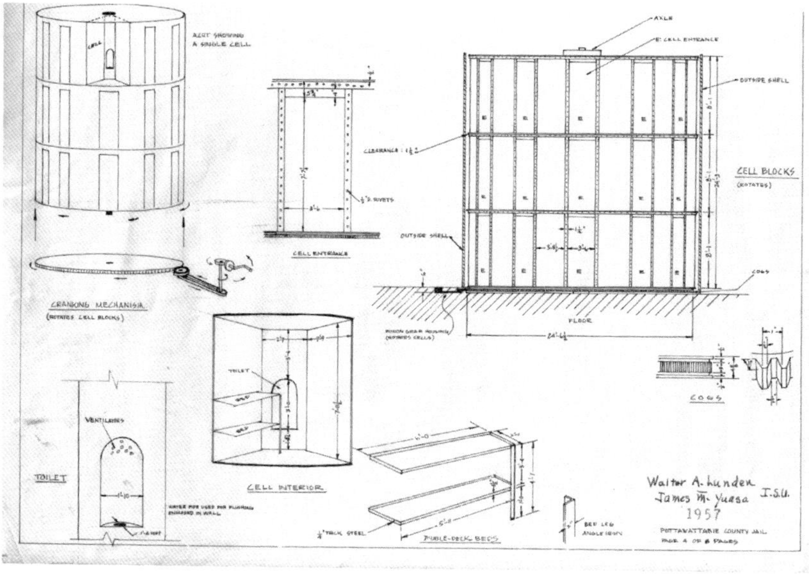

The 1957 plans display the details of the cells and the workings and cogs that turn the rotary device.

Each cell is made up of iron plates and has double bunk beds. At the small end of the pie-shaped cell is a recessed toilet seat, which at one time had a flushing mechanism with water pipes fixed in the central core. Each cell is about eight feet high and seven and one-half feet deep at the center.

All the cells were the same. Each had two bunks and a toilet alcove in the rear of the pie-shaped cell. A wooden bench and electricity were added later.

Prisoners were not able to exit their cells unless their cell was rotated to align with the doorway. The bars in the outer stationary gridded drum covered all of the doorways to the cells in the revolving cylinder. This also made it impossible to see prisoners in other cells.

The inner cylinder with the cells is built around a central axis surrounded by a large tubing or piping. The main axis of this rotary drum rests in a huge collar in the floor and a corresponding collar gives support to the third floor. In order to keep the cylinder in proper alignment a number of large iron casters were inserted beneath the first floor to provide balance during rotation.

Accessible in the basement of the jail is the massive underpinning of the rotation device. These parts were pre-fabricated to the specifications of each jail. The cost of the steel and iron work amounted to $7,350.

Power to rotate the inner cylinder upon the axis and casters is by use of a hand crank device located in a small room outside the area where the unit is located. The hand crank is turned by one man who can easily revolve the cylinder. An advantage to the rotation of the cells, was that the jailer could easily monitor each cell from one vantage point as the cylinder revolved. A note in the patent description from 1881 says that the cylinder could be kept in rotation all through the night when prisoners may not be easily watched, thus, preventing them from cutting their way out of the cells. This was accomplished by using a heavy spring that could be regulated like any clock-works or similar mechanism such as weight driven clocks. This option, however, was not utilized in the Pottawattamie County Jail.

The gears that moved the roundtable of the cells, located in the basement, measure over a foot in diameter.

On each tier of the cell blocks is the crank mechanism, located at the entryway to the cells. A crank handle was inserted and could be turned easily by one man.

To further insure security there was one main passageway from the outside entrance to the inner circular cage. Each prisoner entered through a heavy, screened, sliding door to pass into a small room. Opposite the sliding door was an ingenious swinging door, built like a vertical rocker arm with a segmental gridded frame at the opposite end reaching from floor to ceiling.

When in position one end of the segmental door secures the doorway into the outer stationary shell. In order to open the passageway, the rocker-pivoted door was swung to the right or left which opens both entrances. In this position the prisoner could be taken to the cell or to the exercise area that surrounds the outer stationary shell. After the passage had been gained the rocker arm device was swung back into position and secured by heavy locks secured to the lever and the doorway.

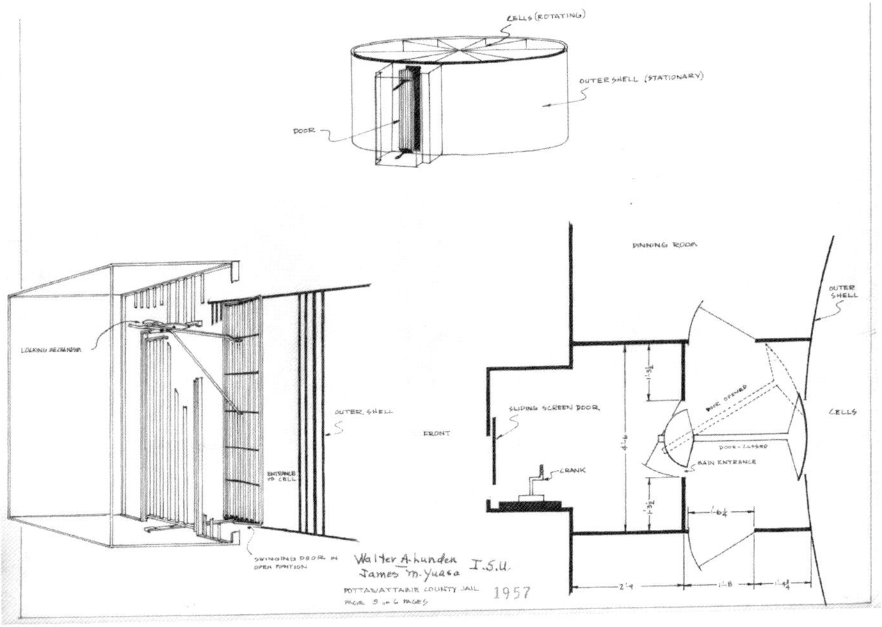

The architectural drawing illustrated the location of the hand crank to turn the rotary mechanism as well as the functionality of the door mechanism's rocker arm. This rocker arm allowed for the security of the jailer to easily handle one prisoner at a time.

Around the outer shell of the rotary device was the exercise area that had a flagstone floor that served as a day room for prisoners. This flagstone flooring has been covered over by cement, though in places the cement is eroding away, and the original flagstone floor is visible. This area provided dining, laundry and bathing facilities as well as benches and tables for the prisoners. The day room has three corner windows and one main window in the west wall. These windows extend to the ceiling with openings in the floors. Each window is covered by a double set of steel bars made of hollow steel piping with an inner steel rod. Originally this inner rod was designed to revolve in order to prevent anyone sawing through the steel pipe.

Prisoners rarely left their cell block or their day room area. Daily rations of food were passed through a small opening near the kitchen near the main entrance to the rotary cell block. These were referred to as "grub holes" and each level had a "grub hole" large enough to slide a tray of food through to the other side.

On each level was a pass-through commonly referred to as a 'grub hole' where the trays of food were passed into the cell block without opening the door to the interior cell area. The chain next to the tray is a fragment of the massive chain used to turn the gears.

Under normal conditions the rotating jail cell unit could house up to sixty prisoners with two men to a cell and a total of ten cells per level, twenty prisoners on each level. However, during the 1932 Farmer's revolt between fifty-five to 165 men were held in the jail for a short period of time. (See chapter III.) This large number of incarcerated men was unprecedented and never repeated. For the majority of the jail's history an average of about twenty-five to thirty prisoners were housed at any given time.

A primary issue for housing prisoners has always been a question of sanitation and dealing with human waste. In this design, the rotary jail had a revolutionary method for handling the problem. This was a time in history when few people had indoor plumbing other than a pump in the kitchen. What the creators of the jail came up with was a remarkable luxury for the era, an ingenious waste system for 1885. Each cell had its own toilet.

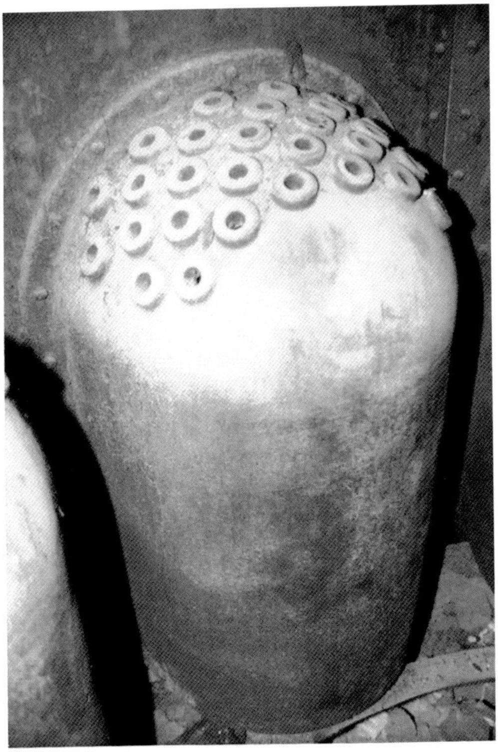

The idea of indoor plumbing was quite revolutionary in 1885 when most people did not have indoor plumbing. This shows the back side of a privy seat in a cell, with ventilation holes in top.

At the small end of each of the wedge-shaped cells was a privy seat. This was an attempt to provide sanitary comfort if not some privacy to the men in their cells. Underneath and inside the privy area, a circular trough was located at each level and water flowed slowly and consistently into a center standpipe. This trickle of water was to keep human waste flushed away. For the most part, it worked remarkably well.

The interior column was set up for sanitation. This photo shows the backs of the toilet alcoves and ventilation holes. They are suspended over the bottom tier cells.

Each of the toilet units had a flush tank with a double flotation device.

Drawbacks to this revolutionary idea was that it didn't work as well as designers had hoped. Too often prisoners would throw wads of paper into the hole in order to make trouble for the jailer who would in turn have to bring a hose and flush out the system.

Almost at the top of the working central core of the sanitation area, looking up at the grid. The iron grids each open to allow access for maintenance.

On the fourth floor, in the center of the warden's living quarters, is the top side of the iron grids. The large wrench is used to open each of the hatches. A prisoner once tried to use this as means of escape. He was quickly discovered and returned to his cell.

The Squirrel Cage Jail was built by the Wickham Brothers of Council Bluffs and the architectural firm Eckel and Aldrich of St Joseph, Missouri. Except for a few changes the jail remains practically unaltered from the time it was built in 1885. A few important upgrades have been installed over the years. The sanitation systems have been upgraded, a heating system was also fitted, and running water and a shower was installed in the 1930's.

Sadly, the original drawings and blueprints for the jail have been lost. However, in 1957, James Yates, while a student at Iowa State College under the supervision of Walter A. Lunden, a professor of sociology, made detailed measurements of the interior of the jail building and rotary unit. Drawings, made by Jim Yuasa, are in the archival collection at the jail. These drawings illustrate the general design and interior measurements of the Squirrel Cage Jail. Yates, however, cautions that there may be some errors, as parts of the building were not accessible for proper measurements.

THE FARMER'S HOLIDAY REBELLION

The great crash of the stock market in October of 1929 plunged the nation into one of the darkest eras in American history. The economic depression affected the entire nation during the 1930's. Money was tight, resources limited, and tempers were taut as people struggled to make ends meet. There was no end in sight to the Great Depression, and the future looked bleak. Bankruptcies and foreclosures were all too common and many farmers fled to the "land of milk and honey": California, only to find the borders guarded and people refused entry. The number of suicides increased dramatically leaving families destitute and distraught. These desperate times across the nation led to a rebellion that broke out across the Midwest. Council Bluffs and the Squirrel Cage Jail played a role in events as they unfolded.

For farmers it was the worst of times; it edged on disaster. By the time the Farmer's Rebellion occurred, farmers had already dealt with more than ten years of depressed prices for their goods, so much so that it cost them more to produce the commodities than they were paid for them. Though the National Farmers Union lobbied for legislation to provide aid and tariff reform, nothing came from their efforts. Farmers were losing money. No longer could they make mortgage or loan payments resulting in their properties being foreclosed upon and their equipment seized.

In late August of 1932 the Farmers' Holiday Association had the idea to organize, taking the form of a "Holiday" from farming. In other words, this "Holiday" asked farmers to stop selling their goods, as well as refrain from purchasing anything for a certain period of time. With this "Holiday" the Association hoped to raise an awareness across the nation of the importance of farm products and purchases.

With farmers in the Midwest and Iowa angry over poor and ever-falling prices they were being paid for their livestock and produce, fifty-five men, primarily farmers, took action. These men began picketing along near-by highways, blocking all roads into Council Bluffs in an effort to stop other farmers who were not participating in the "Holiday" from getting their goods to the Omaha markets.

Picketers gathered at the east and north edges of Council Bluffs. Sheriff Percy Lainson kept a watchful eye on the protesting men, allowing them to picket peacefully. However, the peace didn't last. The picketers blocked Highway 34 into Council Bluffs from the south. When deputy Frank Owens ordered them to move aside and not stand in the road. The protesters refused. They ignored the warning and picketers blocked the highway near the Iowa School for the Deaf using telephone poles to stop the traffic. Sheriff Lainson had these men arrested and brought to the Pottawattamie County Jail. The men detained were charged with unlawful assembly while attempting to keep live-stock and produce trucks from reaching an important Omaha market.

Members of the Farmer's Holiday Rebellion protest on the highway with wires strung across the road, as well as 'stop sticks' crudely made of large nails hammered into a board and placed in the roadway to pop the tires of anyone who dared to cross over them.

Sheriff Lainson continued his operations to keep highways open and directed his deputies to arrest every man found picketing and charge him with unlawful assembly. Forty-nine more picketers were arrested and jailed. Tempers were taut, stretched to the breaking point in both the protesters and the police. Two hundred men resumed their protests. Lainson threatened to hire 5,000 deputies if needed to fight it out as rumors quickly spread that men from "out of town" were assembling in order to aid the picketers and break the arrested protesters out of the "Squirrel Cage" jail. Sheriff Lainson reported if the jail was mobbed his men were armed and would handle it "in the best possible manner." The sheriff issued the special deputies, previously armed only with clubs, with submachine guns, sawed off shot-guns and riot guns. Lainson announced that the deputies armed with submachine guns were authorized to "shoot to kill" if the mob tried to make an assault on the jail.

National newspapers reported the story of the strike on August 26, 1932, as farmers threatened to take over the jail in Council Bluffs demanding the release of their fellow protesters in the Farmer's Strike. F. Raymond Snyder of Kingsley, Iowa was a leader in the protest movement with an aim to increase farm prices by blockading markets. He warned Sheriff P. A. Lainson that if the picketers were not freed from the jail by that evening the farmers would take matters into their own hands and raid the jail and release them.

The curious assemble outside the jail-yard to get a look at the protesting farmers. There was not enough room in the jail to house all the arrested protesting farmers.

Tension crackled on both sides. The Daily Nonpareil published a front-page warning to citizens to stay away from the jail for their own safety.

The Omaha Evening World Herald newspaper fueled the flames of unrest by reporting that a thousand, perhaps two thousand farmers were camped at the edge of the city and more were planning to descend upon Council Bluffs in answer to their fellow protesters who had been arrested and placed in the Squirrel Cage Jail. "They're going to tear down the jail." This rumor spread quickly as the tempers of the men flared along Highway 34 when deputies lobbed tear gas at the protesters hoping to disperse the growing crowd.

In response Sheriff Lainson rounded up more deputies, bringing the number of deputies sworn in to 112 and mobilized them at the courthouse to surround the courthouse and the jail. A hardware store truck delivered baseball bats to deputies, while inside the jail riot gear and machine guns were issued. On the grounds the deputies took practice swings with their newly issued bats as crowds grew to watch the spectacle unfolding. More rumors spread charging the tension even higher. "They say seventy-five trucks jammed with men are coming." "Somebody just saw 1500 men going through Honey Creek." "There are two thousand men out on Highway 34 waiting for the word to mobilize."

There were no farmers or protesters in the crowds around the courthouse and jail. People shuffled nervously, voicing their fears in whispers asking; "What are the farmers doing?" "Where will they strike first?" "How will they approach the jail, from Pearl Street or circle around?" "Will they wait until it is dark to make their move?"

In front of the courthouse in Council Bluffs the curious spectators assemble to witness the arresting and incarceration of the farmers. Rumors spread through the crowds quickly adding to the tensions of the day before a peaceful resolution was reached.

In the midst of the tension a shot rang out, startling the crowds, and bringing them running with more questions on their lips. "Did you hear that? It was a gunshot, wasn't it?" "Where did it come from?" "Where are the farmers?" "What direction will they be coming from?" A new panic gripped the crowds. They had no answers to their questions.

Deputy Sheriff Kinsell had been training the men on the use of their newly issued weapons. He had been showing the men how to use the riot gun and it accidently went off. Kinsell said he didn't know it was loaded. Special Deputy Claude Dail, who lived at 509 Damon Street, fell to the floor, mortally wounded. He was taken to hospital where he died two hours later. Also shot was another special deputy, Joe Ludwig, of 1328 B Street. The bullet hit him in the leg.

The shootings drew even more people and triggered rumors that the war was on. More questions buzzed through the gathering throngs. "How did the farmers hope to take over the jail?" "Can the deputies armed only with baseball bats ever stop five thousand angry protesters?"

At the same time meetings were being held behind closed doors in the courthouse, with the sheriff, county attorney and other officials all hoping to find an amicable solution to the growing problems.

Then, later, the Chamber of Commerce met at the Hotel Chieftan, calling for an emergency "peace conference." The mayor, chief of police and sheriff met with a delegation of nine of the striking farmers. After three- and one-half hours of negotiations the farmers said they would withdraw ninety percent of their men if the sheriff would allow a small group of peaceful protesters to continue without harassment. The National Chairman from the Farm-labor party and an attorney from the Iowa Holiday movement were granted permission to visit the prisoners in the Squirrel Cage Jail and let them know the men were negotiating for their release. Lainson, in agreement with other county officials, agreed to release the prisoners on $100 bonds each and bring them in later for trial. By the next day some of the wealthy farmers had raised the $5,000 bail money to free the farmers held in the jail. Justice Dewitt agreed to accept the bonds for all the forty-seven farmers still being detained. It still took hours to complete the release of the men being held. When it was finally accomplished, they all gathered amicably for photos and newsreel footage to record the event. The entire mood had shifted.

Sheriff Lainson directed the farmers into the jail.

The men were now released on bail. As the imprisoned farmers left the jail a crowd of several hundred spectators and farmers assembled to witness their release. The law officers slowly moved into the courthouse. The crowds paid little attention to law enforcement carrying machine guns, even though the court house was heavily-guarded against the actions of the mob should they become unruly. Pacified by the liberation of their comrades there was no need for the fire power the Sheriff had standing by.

Mayor Myrtue then met with a group of protesting farmers who were south bound into town as they entered city limits. He was able to persuade the group to disperse. Tensions eased and further violence was avoided. As the picketing continued Sheriff Lainson added fifty more special deputies in accordance with the peace conference, these men were to assist the farmers in peaceful protest. One of the major labor unions passed a resolution to support the striking farmers. As a result, many of the union men hired by Sheriff Lainson as special deputies turned in their badges at the courthouse with their resignations. The numbers of deputies and protesters began to moderate.

Businessmen in towns in Western Iowa also met with striking farmers, negotiating better prices for milk; and the sale of cattle at the stockyards, with shipments approved by the Holiday Association and agreements with trucker's associations and Robert's Dairy. Though the protest failed to become a national force for all the improvements they desired, it managed to get authorities to make some changes. Prices were increased and an awareness of the plight of the farmers was brought to the attention of the American people.

Although the farm strike gathered a great deal of media attention, the reality was most farmers didn't participate, prompting radical members of the Association to block roads to keep those still wanting to sell their goods from getting to the markets.

This incident in Council Bluffs did not end the Farmer's Holiday. Not far away near Spencer, Iowa, some 400 farmers gathered on a highway with the intent to resume their picketing. Eric Carlson, who was the leader of this group, had expected a turnout of 1,000 men. Carlson intended to close the city to all incoming shipments of farm livestock and produce. In Sioux City, another group of eighty-eight protesters were released because authorities failed to file any charges against them. The men had been arrested for unlawful assembly in an effort to break the strike and protest activities in that area.

Though strikes continued elsewhere, by the end of August the situation at Council Bluffs was essentially over. The Farmer's Rebellion passed into history. By May of 1934 Congress passed the first farm bill as part of President Roosevelt's New Deal.

SPECIAL DEPUTY CLAUDE B. DAIL

Sergeant Jason LeMaster researched the life and service of Claude Dail for the article he wrote about the Farmer's Holiday. With his permission I have included what he discovered about Special Deputy Dail.

Claude Dail was a veteran of WWI, serving as a private with the 150th Field Artillery. After serving his country overseas, he returned to the United States and eventually moved to Council Bluffs where he lived with his father. Claude served his country valiantly and wanted to continue his service at home. Claude was a Special Deputy for the Pottawattamie County Sheriff's Office for three (3) days, before his untimely death. Claude was survived by his father, Perry N. Dail, of Council Bluffs and his mother, Mrs. Edna Polston, of St. Charles, Missouri.

So now in 2014, we know about "The Farmers Holiday Strike" and the articles that were written of the pressures that farmers felt, the turmoil that resulted, and the tragedies that occurred. We know of Special Deputy Claude B. Dail and his duties to his Country and his willingness to step forward and help his fellow citizens.

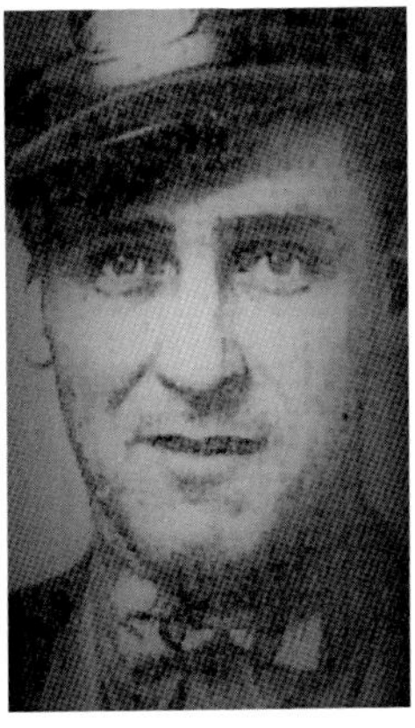

Special Deputy Claude B. Dail, the only member of law enforcement to have lost his life in the Pottawattamie County Jail. He was shot in the abdomen in late August of 1932 when a riot gun accidently discharged.

It is with regret that this story got lost in time. So now, 82 years later, we want to honor your service. The Pottawattamie County Sheriff's Office has been approved to add Special Deputy Claude B. Dail to the National Law Enforcement Memorial Wall in Washington D.C. The name will be formally dedicated on May 13th at the 26th Annual Candlelight Vigil during National Police Week.

The tale of the lone local casualty of the event, Deputy Dail, came to a halt for over eighty years until it was discovered that his name wasn't listed on the National Law Enforcement Memorial Wall in Washington, D.C.. This has been corrected and his name was formally dedicated May 13, 2014 at the 26th Annual Candlelight Vigil during National Police Week. The Historical Society of Pottawattamie County has placed a memorial to all local law enforcement officers and fire fighters who have lost their lives in the line of duty located at the Squirrel Cage Jail Museum, 226 Pearl Street.

INMATES

For the most part, the majority of inmates housed at the Squirrel Cage Jail were petty criminals who served time for vagrancy, breaking and entering, burglary, larceny, forgery, drunkenness, reckless driving, or embezzlement. However, there were others who committed greater crimes of assault, kidnapping, extortion and murder.

Rumor persists that one well known criminal, George Nelson was housed in the Squirrel Cage Jail for a short time, probably when transporting him from one place to another. Though this seems unlikely when one researches the places he robbed, times he was captured and any association with Pottawattamie County.

GEORGE NELSON

Lester Joseph Gillis, known by the alias of George Nelson was also called Baby Face Nelson, yet very few people ever dared to call him that to his face. He was saddled with the moniker because he had such a youthful countenance. He was usually called Jimmy by other members of the criminal ranks. John Dillinger was one of his many associates whom he assisted in a jail break from Crown Point, Indiana earning him the title of Public Enemy Number One.

Did Baby Face Nelson ever spend a night in the Squirrel Cage Jail as a special guest of the Pottawattamie County Sheriff's Police? There are no official records that state that it ever occurred, though it is true that he and his gang robbed the First National Bank in Mason City, Iowa. In the exchange of gunfire, he was wounded, but he was not captured, and made for Reno, Nevada. He spent little time in Iowa during his criminal career.

LESTER GILLIS
AKA
"BABYFACE" NELSON

Lester Joseph Gillis, also known as George Nelson is said to have spent a short time in the Pottawattamie County Jail. Though he was commonly known as Baby Face Nelson, few people dared call him that to his face.

The end of the line for Baby Face Nelson happened in Illinois. November 27, 1934 outside of Chicago in the town of Barrington, Nelson, his wife and John Paul Chase led FBI agents on a wild car chase. Nelson's wife, Helen drove so the men could shoot at their pursuers. She veered into the entrance of Barrington's North Side Park and Stop. She took cover in a ditch while the men had a final shoot-out. Nelson was struck several times, the fatal shot hit him in the abdomen and sliced through his liver. Yet he still fought the agents. Nelson, his wife and Chase managed to get away. He said to his wife "I'm done for." Chase drove and Nelson gave directions to a safe house on Walnut Street in Wilmette. That evening he died of the nine gunshot wounds he'd received in the gunfight.

BROWN AND KELLEY

In February of 1961 Charles Edwin Kelley, age twenty, and Charles Noel Brown, age twenty-eight, made their way to Council Bluffs from Minneapolis, Minnesota where they had just held-up a gas station. Police from Minnesota, Iowa and Nebraska came together to reconstruct the tragic chain of events caused by these two men.

Brown and Kelley were out together, drinking and looking for trouble. In need of some quick cash, they drove to a filling station on Wayzata Boulevard in Minneapolis, Minnesota. They held up the attendant, threatening him with a screwdriver if he did not hand over the till money. They made away with $200 in cash. They proceeded to go to a bar with the intent to rob the place. The bartender and one client were inside when they entered. Brown and Kelley hustled them into the back room and shot them so as to prevent them being identified.

They caught a bus to Omaha. Along with them was Mrs. Josephine Patricia Nesbit, age twenty-three, also of Minnesota. Their crime spree continued. They robbed an Omaha liquor store on Tuesday evening, killing the operator Harry Goldenberg. They had taken him into the back room and told him to turn around. Mr. Goldenberg refused, so Kelley shot him.

The next day they heard radio reports seeking two men in the bar hold-up in Minnesota. Kelley and Brown figured they were "hot" and took a cab with the woman, Josephine Nesbit, across the Missouri River into Council Bluffs. The cab dropped them off at a downtown tavern. They told Josephine to wait for them while they looked for a car. They saw a car pull to the curb near the Post Office at 6th Street and Broadway. Brown pulled out his gun, got into the passenger side, and Kelley hopped in the back seat. Brown told the man, Alvin Emil Koehrsen age fifty-four, and a resident of Walnut, Iowa, to drive as directed.

They didn't go far. Brown had Koehrsen pull to the curb in a dark residential area near 8th Street and 3rd Avenue. Kelley then pushed the man over and got in the front seat to drive. Things didn't go as they planned. Koehrsen tried to escape. They wrestled with him and shot him. The man had gotten a good look at both of them and they did not want to be identified. Back in the car, it failed to start. Kelley and Brown were forced to walk away in search of another vehicle to hijack.

They came across Kenneth Earl Vencel at the supermarket located at 8th Street and First Avenue. Vencel was age thirty-two and resided at 912 Avenue G in Council Bluffs. The gunmen ordered Vencel into his car and had him drive them to 10th Street and Avenue D. When they arrived, the man hopped out of the car and started to run. They shot him several times as he attempted to get inside someplace, anyplace, with an open or unlocked door.

Abandoning their efforts to kill the witness they drove off in Vencel's car and picked up Josephine. The fugitives did not remain free very long. They boarded a bus and both men were taken into custody from the bus in the police roadblock that had been set up on the north edge of Council Bluffs.

Alvin Koehrsen, an Internal Revenue agent, received seven shots. He was taken to Jenny Edmundson Hospital for surgery to remove the slugs. Two days later when Mr. Koehrsen died, murder charges were filed on Brown and Kelley. They were tagged as "Mad Dog Killers" by the local press. Kelley and Brown were held in the city jail on $20,000 bond, each. Mrs. Josephine Patricia Nesbit held on a $1,000 bond was incarcerated in the Squirrel Cage Jail during Kelley's trial. County Attorney Peter J. Peters stated that Josephine Nesbit was no use for them as a witness and had her released. The men were both charged with two counts of assault with intent to do murder. Brown, who had been a Bible salesman, made a statement about the bloody, drunken robbing and killing spree that he and Kelly had in February. He left his pregnant wife and five children when he and Kelley began their rampage. "It's just that I do things when I'm drunk that I would never do any other time." Brown, a soft spoken, shy man, said he wanted to write his story as a lesson to others, but he didn't know where to begin.

"I don't know why I did it myself." Looking back on his life to date he could see a number of places that may have led him to rebel on this rampage. Brown quit school after the eighth-grade. He wondered if he'd gotten more education, maybe he would have done better. He got married at age sixteen. He enlisted in the army at age seventeen and served eighteen months in Germany with the Seventh Armored Division. He recalled that in Germany he began to drink heavily and that he only got into trouble once: a fight with four soldiers where he got a broken leg. As a result of the fight he was busted from a corporal to a private. He did get an honorable discharge. He got in trouble when he passed a forged check for someone else. He served a year in the reformatory at Pendleton, Indiana. When offered a plea deal to name the person who had him pass the bad check, he shrugged. "I could never bring myself to double-cross a friend." He did say that he had done well as a Bible salesman in Wichita.

Both men were sentenced to hang. According to statutes, they had to be executed within twelve to fifteen months of sentencing, pending no appeal. Charles Kelley's hanging was scheduled for September 6, 1962 at the State Penitentiary at Fort Madison. On the gallows he said he was sorry for what he did. Charles Brown was also executed at Fort Madison by hanging July 24, 1962. These men were the last people to be given the death penalty in Iowa. The ropes used in their hanging are a part of the museum's permanent collection, and one of these ropes is currently on display in the second-floor recreational area of the Squirrel Cage Jail.

JAKE BIRD

Probably the most notorious of all the inmates who were housed at the Squirrel Cage Jail was Jake Bird, a black, transient, serial killer who murdered indiscriminately wielding an ax as he made his way back and forth across the nation. His life was aimless as he wandered from state to state indulging himself as a small-time gambler and crap shooter. When that didn't supply sufficient income, he resorted to burglary and murder. It is in his burglaries that he hacked and bludgeoned his victims not wanting witnesses to his crimes.

The exact location is unknown where Bird was born on December 14, 1901. Bird remarked that it was a Louisiana town so small that it didn't have a post office. His troubles began early on in his life. While living in Greenwood, Louisiana he built a nasty reputation with law enforcement. Though he had no formal criminal record at the time, the sheriff of Shreveport, T. R. Hughes, strongly suggested that Bird, not yet nineteen years old, leave the county and not return because of some trouble involving a white woman. This information would come back to haunt him when it surfaced in his trial for the assault on a Carter Lake, Iowa couple.

In Louisiana, Bird had already been in trouble for his "inappropriate" interactions with white people. These inappropriate interactions were not detailed however; at that time in the South, it would have been considered inappropriate for a black man to speak to a white woman or act in any way aggressively toward any white male.

Jake Bird could be called the most notorious of all the prisoners ever housed in the Pottawattamie County Jail. He murdered at least forty-four people across the nation. Bird used the blunt end of an ax as his weapon of preference. Bird was arrested and tried for the attempted murder of Mr. Harold Stribling of Carter Lake after killing three other people the area. He was found guilty and sentenced to thirty years at Fort Madison State Penitentiary.

Taken from the remembrances of inmates and prison records, it was recalled that Bird could be a nasty, aggressive and hostile person, especially at night. It was said that he was manageable by day, yet something would happen to his personality when the sun had set. When incarcerated at Fort Madison in Iowa, Bird was considered to be a bad prisoner and housed in solitary confinement. It was noted that none of the white prisoners would associate with him, and only a few black prisoners would have anything to do with him. In 1924, when he served time in Utah for burglary, Bird attacked a jailer and engineered a jail break. He was quickly captured in Brighton City, Utah. According to the Ogden

Dispatch: "Bird is very quarrelsome and known among his Negro associates as dangerous."

Jake Bird came to the Council Bluffs-Omaha area riding the rails on the east bound Burlington line. The railroads had agents who policed the boxcars and freight lines where hobos would sneak onto the trains without paying a fee. Most were too poor to afford to buy a ticket. People would ride in the freight cars, between the cars or on the roof of the cars. The roof was considered to be dangerous because of low-hanging tree branches and tunnels.

Riding the rails was an adventure to young men, and a necessity for the hobo. Bird was traveling through Nebraska when a railroad special agent for the Burlington line, Conrad Barth, rousted Bird and two other men traveling on the same freight car. Gordon Grigor and James Berwald were both eighteen and sons of wealthy, white families from Cleveland, Ohio. They had decided to travel the country for a vacation, bumming their way around the nation as a lark. Outside of Ashland, Nebraska, Special Agent Barth discovered the three men and ordered them off the train.

They were not willing to go quietly. Barth wrestled with the three men to throw them off the moving train, as was well within his job to do so. In the tussle Grigor fell from the train and slid under the car onto the tracks. Berwald ran off and Bird was struck a number of times. Grigor's legs and a hand were severed when he fell under the wheels of the train. He was taken to the hospital but died of his wounds. Grigor's dying words were, "A --- pushed me under the wheels." Exactly who had pushed him under the wheels was unintelligible. However, a witness was available to tell the tale of the tussle that cost a young man his life.

Jake Bird claimed to see the white man, Railroad Special Agent Conrad Barth, push the boy off the train. His testimony became an important part of the inquest held in Omaha with Bird as the key witness. Because of Bird's statements Barth was held on second degree murder charges. Bird was offered free lodging in the jail in Wahoo, Nebraska, but he thanked officials and commented that it was "too hot" and declined their offer.

It was while waiting to give his testimony that events drastically changed the course of the inquest. With nothing to do in the Omaha area, Bird turned to his usual pleasures of hanging out in low class dives and cabarets where he would gamble, drink and carouse. He made some friends among those who lived in this demi-monde. It would be these friends who would later speak up for Bird.

Probably growing bored, restless and short of cash, Jake Bird resorted to burglary and murder.

November 18, 1928, Bird went on a robbing and killing spree that terrorized the Omaha and Council Bluffs area. Bird entered the home at 4121 North 28th Street, belonging to Mr. J. W. Blackman, a seventy-four year-old expressman, in the predawn hours. He attacked and killed the man before searching the house for anything he could steal. Later that Sunday morning Mr. Blackman's son discovered his father's body. At first his son thought his father was simply sleeping, but soon something didn't seem right to him. His father was too still even for sleep. He raised the blanket where his father lay on the daybed in the living room of the house. To his horror he saw his father covered in blood, his head beaten in while he had been sleeping. When police were called a bloodstained ax was discovered secreted under a pile of wood.

Bird, long gone from this killing, was not yet sated.

Mrs. Walter Russo, age twenty-one and mother of two children, lived with her husband and her sister, Greta Brown, age eighteen, in their south Omaha home on South 41st Street. From the evidence gathered, Bird bided his time, watching the Russo home as Mr. Russo, a milkman with Robert's Dairy, prepared for work, and by 3:00 A.M. exited his home by the back door. Waiting to be sure the man would not return, Bird waited a little longer then made his move. Bird entered the home by the back door that Mr. Russo had exited shortly before and had not bothered to lock.

Armed with his ax, Bird first strangled Mrs. Russo in her bedroom then crushed her skull with an ax, killing her. Next, he smashed in the head of her younger sister who was sleeping upstairs. After the women were dead, he prowled about the house taking items he could easily sell to any fence of stolen goods in the underworld of Omaha. The two young children, Melvin age nine months and Robert age three, who slept in the bedroom with their mother, Mrs. Russo, were left unharmed. According to newspaper accounts, when police came to investigate it was noted that a smear of blood was on Melvin's face.

But it was still not enough for Bird.

The next day, early in the morning of November 19 before the dawn, his need for cash and blood lust had not yet been satisfied. Bird attacked Mr. C. E. Thompson with an empty catsup bottle in his candy store in Omaha. Nothing was taken; however, a neighbor saw a Negro man running away.

While police were investigating the murder of Mr. Blackman, they received word about another two slayings. Mr. Russo had come home from work about 2:00 in the afternoon to find his wife and her sister brutally murdered, their skulls crushed by a blunt instrument. Neither woman had a chance to struggle with their attacker. They were each still lying in their beds, their bodies stripped of their clothing and provocatively arranged. Mr. Russo first entered the bedroom he shared with his wife where he was met by his terrified three-year-old child. The nine-month-old baby still slept in the crib at the bedside. On the second floor he discovered his wife's sister naked, her head bashed in as well. Evidently

Bird had taken the time to gloat over the dead body of the young woman. Horrified by what he witnessed, Mr. Russo quickly covered the body with a comforter before hurrying back down the stairs and out of the house screaming hysterically. A neighbor heard his anguished cries and came out as Mr. Russo fainted on the neighbor's front lawn.

November 20 the killing spree continued just across the Missouri River in Carter Lake, Iowa, though this time his victims survived. Jake Bird staked out another home looking for windows he could pry open, or doors that were unlocked. He found his way into the home of Mr. and Mrs. Harold Stribling and their two children. Upon entering, he listened for sounds of disturbances, and for where the residents were slumbering. He silently crept into the bedroom where the couple were sleeping. Raising up the blunt end of his weapon, an ax, he repeatedly brought it down on the head of Mr. Stribling, half hauling the man out of his bed and onto the floor. He left Mr. Stribling for dead, for he would have awakened Mrs. Stribling by then, and needed to deal with her immediately.

Mrs. Stribling gave a chilling account of her ordeal.

Bird beat Mr. Stribling in the bed with the blunt end of the ax, leaving him on the floor with his skull fractured.

Bird, having dispatched Mr. Stribling to an unconscious state, leaving him for dead and assured of Mrs. Stribling's compliance for the moment, proceeded to walk into the bathroom, turn on the light and wash his hands, deliberately and slowly. As he did, he asked her if she had children. His question chilled her to the bone. He dried his hands now with as much care. She said, yes, she had children. Bird turned to her and demanded to see the sixteen-month-old child. Trembling with fear for what he may do next, she reluctantly took him to see where the baby was sleeping. Bird stared down at the sleeping infant as if transfixed. He never touched the child, but soon came out of his trance, turned to face her and grabbed Mrs. Stribling.

Bird dragged Mrs. Stribling out of the house, and down the dark streets of Omaha, into the woods and the swamps, all the while beating her so badly her eyes were damaged. She tried to get away from him a number of times, but he managed to overcome her and beat her some more, hauling her ever deeper into the swamplands below Omaha.

She pleaded with Bird to spare her life. She promised him she would not call the police or detectives immediately upon release. He would not let her go. He forced her to come with him into the weeds and swamps of South Omaha

When she finally managed to escape his grasp, she hid in the weeds. She could hear him looking for her in the darkness of the early morning before the sun began to rise. When she thought he was far enough away she emerged from the swampy area looking bloody, bruised and quite disheveled in her nightgown and encountered a policeman from the bottomland thickets near 5th and Locust Streets. It was now about 4:00 A. M. and the dawn was just beginning to color the skies when she encountered the policeman on his rounds. She was taken immediately to the Lord Lister Hospital at 26th Street and Dewey in Omaha and interviewed by police, who obtained a description of events and of the man who attacked her and her husband.

Headlines tell a horrific tale. Two women attacked in East Omaha. Murderer kills two, stripping them. Spares the life of the next victim. It was the survivor who gave police a vivid description, Mrs. Stribling. Mrs. Stribling described a well-dressed Negro, young, about twenty-one or twenty-two. Height five foot, seven inches, weighing about 140 pounds. His skin was medium-colored, he did not have very kinky hair. He was wearing a dark suit, probably gray, neatly pressed and there was a good crease in the trousers. On his head he wore a dark gray cap, and he also sported a bow tie and an overcoat.

More than 500 police officers, railroad detectives and civilians searched for the hatchet man in Omaha and across the Missouri River in Council Bluffs. The areas searched included the bottomlands of South Omaha where the killer may have crossed the Illinois Central Railroad bridge into Iowa. The search spread across both sides of the river.

Police picked up a man carrying a broken hatchet, Cecil Casafax, who was held and interrogated. He said that he found it on the way home, picked it up thinking he could use it. Police were not convinced that Casafax was the killer they sought. He was released. Police and railroad detectives urged people to stay inside and lock their doors.

Bird was in Omaha still waiting to testify at the inquest for Gordon Grigor's death when he was arrested for the assault on Mrs. Stribling. When she made a positive identification of Bird, there were some whispered accusations of revenge against Bird for his testimony against Railroad Special Agent Barth for implicating him in Grigor's death. These accusations were quickly dismissed as evidence mounted against Jake Bird.

Bird protested his innocence and claimed to be at one of his gambling haunts on the night in question. According to Bird he went downtown about 2:30 and had a barbeque sandwich. Then he went home before he headed out again to play some pool and gamble in an Omaha cabaret. From there he went to Sioux City, but didn't stay long when he heard the description of the perpetrator of the Stribling attempted murders.

November 21, 1928 police set up a dragnet hoping to catch the guilty person.

Soon upon his return Bird was picked up by Omaha police who rounded up the usual suspects. However, he was held only an hour before being let go due to a misunderstanding in the description.

Mrs. Stribling's description of the man who "attacked my husband and me was a slick Negro." Those sending out descriptions of her attacker misconstrued her words to say the man had slick hair and Brilliantine. The clothing the man wore was accurately passed on: an overcoat, suit and cap.

On November 22, 1928 Jake Bird was caught.

Police had searched diligently for this fiendish attacker. They combed the swamplands and weeds by the old box factory in South Omaha for more clues of what occurred in the abduction of Mrs. Stribling. Bird remained incarcerated in the Iowa County Jail, not yet charged with any crime. He claimed he was innocent. He said he had been gambling in a cabaret, and he had friends who could alibi him for the time of the crime.

Police took Bird to Mrs. Stribling's hospital room to see if she could identify him as her attacker.

"As sure as there is a God in heaven, Jake Bird, you are the man," Mrs. Stribling said. "I kept my word with you. I didn't call detectives at once, but they have caught you in spite of that. You know that I know you are the man, Bird. Why don't you tell the truth to the officers, it will go easier for you?" Mrs. Stribling said calmly.

"Lady, I never saw you before in my life," Bird replied.

"Are you sorry for what you did that night?" Mrs. Stribling fired back at Bird.

"I don't know what you are talking about, lady." Bird said back to her, still maintaining his innocence.

Bird's landlady testified for him. Also, twenty friends testified that Bird was, indeed, with them. However much of their testimony was contradictory.

Bird was held in an Iowa jail; however, the location was not named in the press for fear of mob violence against Bird. Northrup, the Pottawattamie County Attorney, presented the case to a grand jury in early January of 1929. It did not take long for the grand jury to render a decision to proceed with the case against Jake Bird for the assault on Mr. Stribling. Northrup planned to prosecute the attack upon Mrs. Stribling separately and at a later date.

Police pieced together Bird's *modus operandi*. In the small hours of the night, Bird stakes out a house. He looks for a way in, often finding people did not lock their doors. He makes his way, silently into the room where people are sleeping and dispatches them quickly with smashing blows to their heads, beating them in a violent frenzy with the back of an ax or other blunt instrument, crushing their skulls.

Jake Bird showed a bit of a nervous reaction when he was informed about the fingerprints taken from the scene of the crime in the Stribling home. Authorities needed to rule out whether they were Bird's or members of the ambulance crew. Police found incomplete finger and palm prints on the walls and woodwork of the Stribling home, in particular, in the bedroom. When he was informed, he showed the first emotion to interrogators by dropping his steady gaze as he began to fumble for words. He glanced at his accuser then looked quickly away.

"The fingerprints obtained in the Stribling home would tell the story of the murder better than anything else on earth could do," the interrogator stated.

"And they got them prints?" Bird asked anxiously.

A reporter from the Nonpareil heard some of the evidence and interviewed Jake Bird, then cobbled together a chain of events in the Stribling home for a lurid article in the newspaper. The trail of fingerprint evidence revealed that the intruder entered the house from a sloping cellar door into the basement. Then the intruder felt his way in the darkness, leaving his mark on the wall. The man lit a match, found a trapdoor, but could not open it. Next the intruder tried to push open a trapdoor in the kitchen floor to gain access to the main house. This door was locked. The intruder left some very clear marks in that basement. In the basement he saw a hatchet and took it. Crawling back out of the basement, he next tried to gain access via the back door of the home. Upon entering the house, he listened for the sounds of the residents slumbering. The kitchen was next door to the bedroom. He entered the bedroom raised the hatchet and struck the sleeping Mr. Stribling three times. The reporter stated that as he reconstructed the events of the home invasion to the prisoner, Bird enjoyed the telling of the crime. Bird commented that he would have killed Mrs. Stribling if he had been the burglar, then there wouldn't be any descriptions going around.

As a result of his arrest for the assault on Mr. Stribling and the kidnapping of Mrs. Stribling, Bird's testimony on the case against Special Agent Conrad Barth for the death of Gordon Grigor, was greatly, if not wholly discredited and all charges against Barth were dropped.

As police delved into the life history of Jake Bird, a troubled and violent past began to emerge. Police across the nation had an interest in capturing and punishing him. Reports come in from across the country relating to the long history of crime and violence perpetrated by Jake Bird.

A record surfaced of Bird being released from a Los Angeles jail July 6, 1920 after a hearing on a robbery charge. In 1922, Bird was arrested in Los Angeles, California for impersonating an officer. He served a short jail sentence, also in Los Angeles for the theft of $3.00. A record is also on the books of his arrest, dated November 22, 1922, in Oakland, California.

In 1924 Bird was twice arrested in Salt Lake City on burglary charges. He claimed to know nothing about it. Bird managed to escape from the Utah prison. Mr. D. Brown, a former member of the Ogden, Utah police recalled that Jake Bird, age twenty-four, was at one time an Ogden city undercover man. Bird worked for the city by day, yet at night he resorted to old habits and robbing houses. He was finally arrested for robbing the home of Mrs. Pearl Wheatly, who resided on Horton Avenue. Bird served a term for second degree burglary and was released January 15, 1927.

Upon seeing the newspaper accounts of the case against Jake Bird for the attempted murder of Mr. Stribling, the sheriff in Chickasha, Oklahoma believed that Jake Bird was the man who, a little over a year previously, in 1927 killed another man's wife by stabbing her in the back. Bird was sentenced and incarcerated in the State Hospital for the Criminally Insane in Norman, Oklahoma. While in the custody in the hospital the prisoner said he was from Omaha. He claimed to sleep during the day and "played nights" frequenting the cabarets during his stay in Omaha. Bird escaped from the institution. When Bird's description was compared and photos checked to those of the escaped prisoner from the Oklahoma institution, Oklahoma law enforcement believed it was the same man. When Bird was questioned about this he denied ever being in Oklahoma.

A statement about Bird appeared in the November 20, 1928 Council Bluffs Nonpareil newspaper. "His depravity is probably excited by the first vicious attack and thereafter he indulges in his particular vice unmindful of the life or lives he has taken." The women would be stripped, and sometimes placed in revealing poses after death. Police believe that after reconstructing the account from Mrs. Stribling and evidence found at the scene, and in the other two homes of victims that her attacker also broke in and killed the two women in South Omaha, as well as the aged man, Mr. Blackman.

One thing about Bird is revealing. He never molested or injured children. Mrs. Stribling seemed to sense that Bird came out of his killing frenzy as he stood transfixed, gazing at her sleeping child. The two children of Mrs. Walter Russo, one of the South Omaha women killed, were not molested, but her adult sister, Greta Brown, was slain and posed provocatively.

Former Nebraska Douglas County Attorney, A.V. Shotwell had the task of defending Bird at the assault trial. Bird had requested Shotwell because he had assisted in the prosecution of Special Agent Conrad Barth in the death of Gordon Grigor. Shotwell's defense was unsuccessful, even though the landlady of the boarding house and some twenty friends of Bird's testified for him, giving him an alibi for the times in question. However, their testimony contradicted one another's. While Bird was incarcerated in the Squirrel Cage Jail, awaiting his trial for the attack and kidnapping of Mrs. Stribling, Shotwell informed Bird he would not defend him in the second trial, claiming that the work was too great a burden for the small fee he would earn. Richard J. Organ of Missouri Valley was left to defend Bird in his second trial for the assault on Mrs. Stribling. This case never came to trial.

Jake Bird was convicted February 3, 1929 of the assault and attempted murder of Mr. Stribling. He was given the inmate number 14314 as he was sentenced to serve 30-years in the state penitentiary at Fort Madison, Iowa for assault with a hatchet upon Harold Stribling of East Omaha. A $500 reward had been offered, and Bird wrote to the county attorney Henry Beal to protest the awarding of the reward to Steve Maloney, claiming that he was framed. The assault had been committed in Pottawattamie County, and Bird was tried in the district court and convicted by a jury. It was during this time he was incarcerated at the Squirrel Cage Jail. Jake Bird claimed that if this reward was paid it would encourage the framing of other people for crimes they didn't commit.

December 30, 1941 the Nonpareil reported that Jake Bird had been freed from Fort Madison State Penitentiary in Iowa for good behavior and time earned. Charles C. Lacy, clerk of the district court gave the notice of the discharge of the prisoner Jake Bird. His original sentence was thirty years beginning April 25, 1929. Bird had been convicted of the charge of assault with the intent to commit murder with a hatchet of Mr. Harold Stribling in his Carter Lake home.

Out of prison Bird continued to rob and kill people across the United States. In 1943 Bird was arrested in Michigan for a series of burglaries. He pled guilty and sentenced to five years. Released from that stint in prison, Bird made his way to Washington State where he committed his last act of savagery before being apprehended.

In Tacoma, Washington on October 30, 1947 a neighbor heard screams coming from the home of the widow Mrs. Bertha Kludt and called the police. As police arrived, they saw a man running from the house, gave chase and, after a struggle, subdued him. Jake Bird was brought in for questioning but wasn't charged with anything at that time. Police then investigated the Kludt home, discovering a savage attack had been perpetrated upon Mrs. Kludt, age fifty-three, and her daughter Beverly, age seventeen. Both had been beaten and their heads bashed in with an ax.

Bird claimed he was innocent. When he was charged with first degree murder for the killings, he was informed that this charge meant he was facing the death penalty. Faced with a premeditated murder charge, he admitted his guilt in the crime but claimed it was a burglary gone wrong. The women had discovered him, and he told them he would go quietly, but they were screaming and struggled with him. He knocked them down and "just kept swinging" the ax.

Bird offered information that would clear up some other ax murders in the Midwest in hopes of getting his death sentence commuted to life in prison. Among the murders he admitted to were three in Omaha in 1928. He also confessed to one in Tulsa, Oklahoma in 1943 and another in Ogden, Utah in 1947.

Jake Bird was brought to trial, charged with murder in the first degree. On November 24, 1947 the jury had heard the case and retired to deliberate their verdict. It took them thirty-five minutes to come back with a verdict of guilty and the recommendation that he should hang.

After his conviction Bird was sentenced to be taken to the gallows in Walla Walla, Washington, and hanged by the neck until dead. After the sentence was pronounced, Bird was allowed to make a final statement. He spoke for twenty minutes, noting that his request to represent himself had been denied and that his own lawyers were against him. In his final statements after being condemned to death, Bird cursed those who were involved in his trial. "I'm putting the Jake Bird hex on all of you guys who had anything to do with his case are going to die before I do!" Bird added, "You wait and see, you judges and police will be sitting and waiting at the Pearly Gates a long time before I roll up."

Curse or coincidence?

Within a short time six people connected to this trial died. Superior Court Judge E. D. Hodge died suddenly within a month of sentencing Bird. He had conducted Bird's trial in Washington State. Chief Deputy Clerk Ray Clark had handled the paperwork that needed to be filed for the case to go to trial. Joe Karpach was the Pierce County Undersheriff who coaxed twelve confessions for ax murders out of Jake Bird. He died of a heart attack. Tacoma Police Lieutenant Sherman Lyons, who also managed to get confessions from Jake Bird about ax murders, including the murder of Mrs. Kludt and her daughter, also died of a heart attack. It was reported that J. W. Selden, age seventy-five, the lawyer who defended Bird, died on the one-month anniversary of sentencing. He was found sitting at his desk. He also died of a heart attack. Selden was the fifth person to die so far since Bird put his hex on those involved with his punishment. When Bird was informed, he said, "The Bible say rejoice when anyone dies, feel bad when anyone is born."

Bird spent a total of three months maximum time at the jail to await trial and sentencing before being sent to Tacoma, Washington. For the most part Bird was, during the day, considered to be socially all right but, after dark, his behavior was a totally different story. In the night he would scream: "Bring me buckets of blood."

J. W. Selden, the public defender for Bird for the Tacoma killings, made a statement after Bird's conviction. As he filed a motion for a new trial he said, "I feel whenever any man forty-five years old gets an idea that no lives are safe to anyone, except his own, that man is a detriment to society and should be obliterated."

Bird had little formal education but was able to prolong his life for nearly two years with legal maneuvers through the courts in an attempt to postpone his death, trying every legal maneuver and appeal to delay the ultimate fulfillment of his sentence. With partial confessions, he continued to hint to law enforcement that he would be able to assist in helping resolve a large number of unsolved cases. Ultimately, Bird stunned law enforcement officials when he confessed that he knew about or took part in at least forty-four killings. Listed in the states where he had killed were Washington, Colorado, Florida, Illinois, Iowa, Kansas, Kentucky, Michigan, Nebraska, New Jersey, Ohio, Oklahoma, South Dakota and Wisconsin.

Bird admitted to slaying Mrs. Kludt and her daughter, to three murders in Omaha in November of 1928, three in South Bend, Indiana in September of 1942, one in Ogden, Utah October 3, 1947, and one in Highland Park, Illinois on June 24, 1942. He confessed to another in

Evanston, Illinois where he killed Mrs. Lillian Galvin, age forty-five, and her maid Edna Sibilski, age thirty, in a robbery on October 22, 1942. Bird also claimed taking part in other slayings in New Jersey, Illinois and Racine, Wisconsin. These killings were confirmed by Law Enforcement. Investigation into his confessions led to the solving of eleven murders in Iowa, Colorado, Utah, Indiana, Illinois, Nebraska and Washington.

He managed to buy two years before he had exhausted his appeals, his last one turned down hours before his scheduled hanging. On the day before his hanging, the United States Supreme Court rejected Bird's appeal for a review of his case. This was the third time he had been turned down. Previously he had appealed his case four times to the state supreme court, twice to the federal district court, and six times to state superior courts.

An article in the Council Bluffs Nonpareil dated Friday, July 15, 1949, reported that Jake Bird finally met his death that day upon the gallows in Walla Walla, Washington for the ax murders of Mrs. Bertha Kludt and her daughter, Beverly, in Tacoma, Washington on October 30, 1947.

The article went on to report that Bird walked to the gallows in the Washington state penitentiary looking reasonably calm, needing only a slight assistance from two guards. He had no last words to say to the crowd of over 100 people assembled to witness his death. He only made one guttural, unintelligible remark to one of the guards. Reverend Arvid Ohrnell read a note written by Bird stating that he bore no malice to anyone and asked forgiveness. Before the minister had finished reading the note, the trap on the gallows was sprung at 12:06 A M. Fourteen minutes later the prison physician pronounced Bird dead.

At his death his personal fortune amounted to $6.15, which he willed to his attorney Murray Taggart. In his last days Bird spoke of a little black box where he had stashed the ill-gotten gains from his burglaries. He claimed it was in the possession of a friend in Los Angeles, California, yet he never identified this friend. The stolen items were never located.

In his last days he wrote his memoirs which were supposedly turned over to his attorney after his death for publication. No such work has ever come to light as having been published.

Mr. Stribling recovered though he suffered from an indentation in his skull from the blows rained down upon him by Jake Bird. Choosing not to remain in Omaha the Stribling family relocated to Piedmont, California where he worked for an insurance agency. On the morning of February 11, 1959, Mrs. Stribling called her doctor complaining of a severe headache. In the call she also related that she wasn't able to awaken her husband.

When the doctor came to their home, gaining access by the help of a neighbor since no one answered the door, Mr. and Mrs. Stribling were found unconscious. Mr. Stribling died shortly thereafter, while Mrs. Stribling was taken to the hospital and treated for a gunshot wound to the head. When police interviewed her, she stated that she had no recollection of being shot.

Piecing events and evidence together, Mr. Stribling had taken a gun, shot his wife then shot himself. Mrs. Stribling lived on after her husband's death for nearly twenty years. She died in March of 1977.

Not every inmate at the Squirrel Cage Jail can claim a notorious past like Jake Bird. But each man and woman who served their time in the Pottawattamie County Jail would not forget their time there. One prisoner begged to be placed in any other jail in the nation, he even said he would double his sentence if he could serve elsewhere because the nightmare of isolation in a cell on the great rotary wheel was a horrific experience.

RAY L. MARTIN

In early September of 1925, motorist Ray L. Martin was arrested for speeding, and for reckless and intoxicated driving. He could easily have paid his fine of $500.00 yet chose to be remanded to the custody of the county for six months. Martin was the heir to over a million dollars and was the son-in-law of the late multi-millionaire Jacob Krug of Omaha who built a brewery empire. Martin was photographed in the jail while he served his sentence.

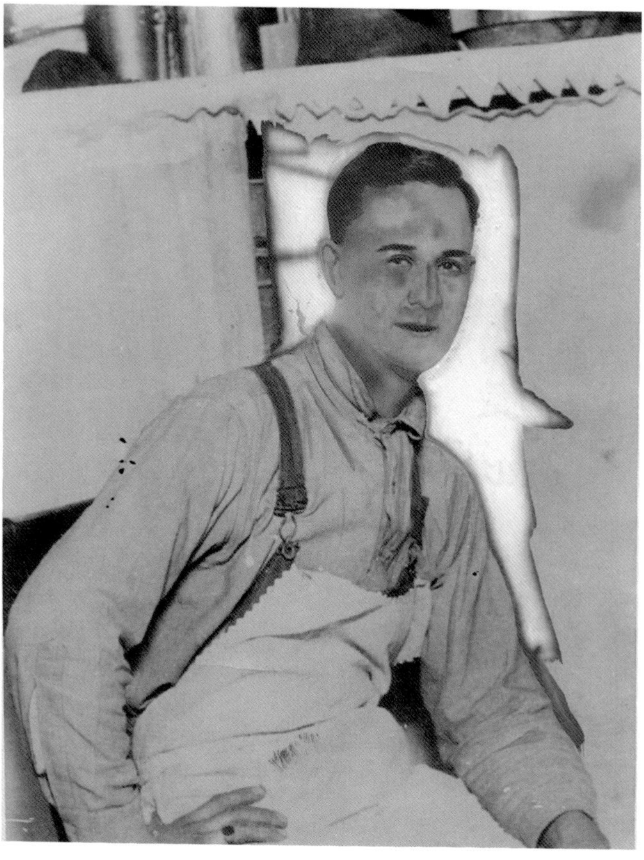

Arrested for reckless driving, Ray Martin preferred to stay in jail instead of deal with his wife. He became a trusty and was housed with another trusty in the basement cell of the jail. He stayed in his bunk while his fellow prisoner escaped.

Ray Martin was awarded the designation of trusty while serving his sentence. This meant he had privileges and freedom most other prisoners did not experience. Instead of having a cell on the first level of the rotary jail, he was housed with another trusty, Carl Edward Johnson in the cell in the basement of the jail located below the dining area. Part of his responsibilities consisted of assisting in the kitchen, and delivery of the meals to the other prisoners through the grub holes on each level. Ray Martin stayed in his bunk even while his cellmate Carl Johnson escaped from the jail. Martin preferred to remain, his sentence would soon be completed within another three months. There was little to lure him from his preferred incarceration.

Within a year after Ray Martin chose to be remanded to the custody of the county jail, his wife sued for divorce. Mrs. Clarabelle Krug Martin was the daughter of the late Jacob Krug the wealthy Omaha brewer. Not wanting his wife to come and bail him out, Martin explained, "I didn't want to be reminded of the favor after I got out."

Mrs. Martin complained that her husband did not work anymore after the experience. He agreed to the divorce and said he would leave town. She asked for custody of Ray Jr., their one-year old child. It was rumored she gave him a property settlement, but she denied this. He was allowed to keep his car. They were married in 1922 after a two-year courtship while he was a baker. Clarabelle and her son moved in with her mother at 1314 South 13th Street.

LYLE ERWIN

A man who gave the name of Lyle Erwin to police was captured on Highway 34, two miles south of Council Bluffs in the early hours of the morning of June 27, 1934. He claimed to be walking back to Council Bluffs after a visit to Red Oak to call upon a married lady by the name of Maxine. He had gotten a ride part of the way back but, for some reason the driver became afraid and let him out at the side of the highway. He continued to walk to Council Bluffs taking some three hours to meander a few miles.

This was the same time that the Police and Department of Justice had staked out an area of Highway 34 as a drop location for an extortion threat made against Earl E. May, of Shenandoah, Iowa. Law enforcement had laid out an elaborate trap to catch the extortionist.

Lyle Erwin tied to justify his presence at the scene and his actions. He said that he had noticed a car slow down, and a man get out and place a package by the side of the road. After the man left, he emerged from the darkness where he had hidden himself and retrieved the package. Federal and State agents were upon him in no time. Police did not believe that he gave his real name, believing Lyle Erwin was an assumed name given in order to evade detection of any other past crimes. Police noted that Erwin, age forty-two, was fairly well dressed and appeared to be well educated. Erwin evidently told the police that he, at one time, had studied medicine.

Lyle Erwin protested his innocence in the matter of the extortion. He claimed that his curiosity was aroused upon seeing the man place the package on the side of the road. Police didn't believe him. His story of walking back from Red Oak did not add up in the time frame he stated, and he was taken to Council Bluffs for further questioning. He was arraigned under the Lindbergh Law for an attempt to extort $6,000 from Earl E. May, a wealthy nurseryman and merchant of Shenandoah, Iowa.

Erwin pled not guilty, and his bond was set at $25,000. Since he was unable to pay his bail, he was remanded to the Pottawattamie County Jail. There he would be housed until a grand jury could be convened for their scheduled session in October. Erwin expressed the hope that police would continue to investigate the extortion plot and find he had nothing to do with it. He stated that he was simply a victim of circumstances. If convicted, the Lindbergh Law carries a sentence up to life.

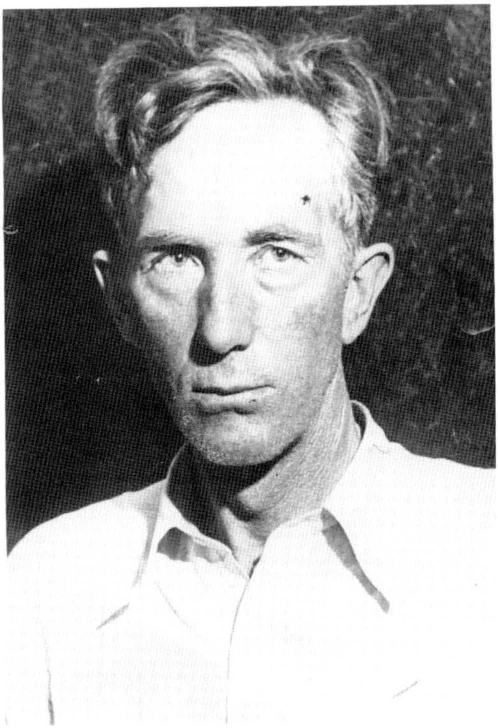

Was Lyle Erwin unlucky in that he was at the wrong place at the wrong time? Or was he guilty of the crime of trying to extort money from Earl E. May of Shenandoah, Iowa? Housed at the Pottawattamie County Jail during his trial, Lyle Erwin was found guilty on one of three counts of extortion.

Erwin said he was an itinerant salesman and told police he had moved to Omaha from Kansas City a week previously. Erwin was pretty much a self-educated man, having only completed his formal schooling through the fifth grade. However, he was an avid reader, mostly reading technical books to fit himself out as a vacuum salesman instead of just selling books.

The charges he faced were based on a series of three letters that had been delivered by mail to Mr. May. These letters threatened Earl May and members of his family unless demands were met. The letter writer threatened to bomb the May's home. The first of these letters directed May to reply by placing an ad in the newspaper want-ads stating, "I will deliver, Earl." Then May was to drive to Omaha by way of Sidney and Glenwood, Iowa. At the side of the road he would see a red flare at the right side of the road. He was to stop, get out and follow the directions as to placing the package of money.

The letter arrived too late for May to place the requested reply in the newspaper. Another letter came on Monday that set up the drop for Tuesday, however a heavy rainstorm interfered. On Thursday another letter arrived, which read:

> *Due to circumstances over which we have no control, we were unable to contact you Thursday PM. Understand you were on the road so credit you with trying to fill your part of the bargain. Now on Thursday, June 21, you are to leave Shenandoah at 8:30 pm. Watch at all times for a red spotlight on the right side of the pavement. Your car identified by green right-hand headlight 6-inch squares of paper on door glasses both sides of car. Manage also to light the inside of your car so we can recognize you readily. Follow instructions given in other letter regarding money $6,000 in used currency, broken series, $5 and $10 notes. 80 per cent to be in $10's.*

As part of the sting, Officer Joseph Burke impersonated Mr. May since he bore a close resemblance to the nurseryman. Burke drove to the site where the threatening letters had instructed. He drove to Omaha and then turned about and came back to the Council Bluffs area. Burke saw a flashlight with red paper over the lens. As he slowed the car the two agents who had been crouching down in the back slipped from the car under the cover of the darkness of the night. Burke stopped the car, got out and found the instructions for what to do next. It instructed him to leave the money by a phone pole across the road and to take the flashlight with it. Burke placed the package as he'd been instructed. Burke got back in the car and drove a little way down the highway before turning around and returning to the scene where the two agents had a man held at gunpoint. The man was Lyle Erwin.

The grand jury convened on September 27, 1934. Lyle Erwin faced three charges, one for each letter. Expert witness testimony was presented comparing Lyle's handwriting to that of the letters. The expert for the prosecution found the handwriting very similar, while the expert for the defense found little in common. As a result, Lyle was only convicted on one of the three counts of attempting to extort $6,000 from Earl E. May. Lyle Erwin was sentenced to serve five years in the Leavenworth Penitentiary.

BERNARD F. SMITH

A story in the Nonpareil of August 9, 1945 reported that Bernard Smith of Oakland California, age thirty-three, would spend time in the Squirrel Cage Jail after his arrest for allegedly kidnapping his estranged wife, Isabelle, also age thirty-three, from her home at 1808 Burt Street in Omaha. He faced charges of robbery with aggravation and with armed intent to use same unlawfully.

Allegedly Smith harmed his wife before he was overtaken by police. Mrs. Smith was in an Omaha hospital suffering from a bullet wound in her knee.

Smith stood before the bench where the judge dismissed the charge of robbery with aggravation. The judge ordered the preparation of two new charges: assault with intent to do great bodily injury and kidnapping. John Tinley represented Smith as defense counsel.

Smith was also named in federal kidnapping charges filed, under the Lindbergh Law. Smith, if convicted, might have faced the death penalty because he was said to have transported Mrs. Smith over the state line between Omaha, Nebraska and Council Bluffs, Iowa. Also, Smith forced Sam Lalich, of 2182 Avenue H, a bridge attendant at the Ak-Sar-Ben bridge, to give up his gun. Smith made his demand for the gun while pointing his own gun at Lalich. He complied. Smith then forced Clifford Donelson, address 204 South 24th Street in Council Bluffs, age thirty-three, to drive his car over the bridge to the city of Council Bluffs.

Smith pled guilty and on October 26, 1945 he was sentenced to a six-month term in the Pottawattamie County jail.

Bernard Smith allegedly kidnapped his estranged wife, and while doing so shot her in the knee. He stole a car and forced the Ak-Sar-Ben bridge attendant to give up his gun. He pled guilty and served a six-month sentence at the Pottawattamie County Jail.

KENNETH LEE HODGE

Twenty-eight-year-old Kenneth Lee Hodge, of 1325 South 10th Street, claimed that he wasn't sure if he was involved in the murder of Harry Minds, age sixty, of 100 North Avenue, on December 25, 1958. Minds was in the habit of carrying large sums of cash. His wallet was not found on his body; however, $426 was discovered under his body when it was removed. Minds was found Christmas evening in the greenhouses of J. F. Wilcox and Sons at 1132 East Pierce Street where he had worked for many years. The Coroner Henry Meyer ruled the death as murder and reported that Minds had been bludgeoned with a thirty-inch piece of steel pipe. He was hit on top of the head at least three times.

The night watchman, Paul Stansberry, of 115 North Avenue, reported to work at 5:30 P. M. and later found the body about 6:30 P.M. face down, lying over a seven-inch steam pipe. Usually Minds gave him a report on temperatures in the greenhouses before heading home for the evening.

Police located the murder weapon in a nearby bed of roses, covered in blood and hair. There was little sign of a struggle, showing that Minds was unaware of his assailant before being struck in the head. Minds had worked at the greenhouse since 1928. His duties included making regular rounds to regulate the temperatures in the greenhouses that were maintained by the boiler.

Hodge claimed to have suffered black out spells ever since he served in Korea in the army, and this was why he was unable to recollect where he had been between 2:30 P. M. and 5 P. M. on the day of the murder. Blood stained clothing was found in Hodge's home when police searched. Hodge was unable to tell police how the blood had gotten onto his clothing.

Witnesses reported that Hodge had been with Minds earlier in the day. Police focused on Hodge as their primary suspect.

Hodge pleaded innocent to the charge of first-degree murder and was held without bond. Twenty-nine hours after Mind's body was discovered, Hodge signed a confession of guilt, admitting that he had bludgeoned Harry Minds on Christmas afternoon. This statement was made to Police Chief B. E. Montgomery and County Attorney Matt Walsh. Hodge stated that the had gone to the greenhouse about 2 P. M. Christmas day to help Minds open the air vents in the greenhouse where the murder occurred.

"When we came to the end of the aisle, I hit Harry with a pipe I'd picked up." Hodge stated in his confession. "I took the billfold from his left rear pocket and went over the hill, back of the greenhouse."

Hodge led police to a terrace behind Hoover School where he had discarded the billfold. Police found $2 still in the wallet.

Hodge related that he had been in an argument with his wife earlier, the day before Christmas. She asked him to get presents for their three children and he refused to buy any presents until he was out of debt. A witness, Joe Tobin, of 104 North Avenue, who was a fireman at the Wilcox Greenhouses, recalled that Minds was a little wary of Hodge as he had attempted to borrow money from him. Hodge had only been employed at the greenhouse for three weeks. Tobin also told police that Minds planned to take his money home and leave only $2 in his wallet. Police theorized that Minds had taken the wad of cash from his wallet, leaving only the $2 in it, and stuffed the cash in his shirt pocket. That was before he was bludgeoned and fell to the ground; the cash had fallen under his body, unseen by his attacker.

Hodge was housed at the Pottawattamie County Jail during his trial. The case was tried in twelve court-day sessions that spread over two and a half weeks. John Peters, Hodge's defense attorney, argued that the state prosecuted the wrong man stressing that police had not done a thorough investigation. He argued that police failed to get a match of Minds' blood, and the blood found on Hodge's clothing. He even claimed that police planted evidence since they did not find the bloody clothing until the third search of the Hodge's home. Peters had also tried to use an insanity plea, citing the blackouts Hodge had suffered for years.

The prosecuting attorney, Deputy Assistant County Attorney Ross Canigilia kept his summation short. "There is but one man in this courtroom who knows what happened December twenty-fifth. That man is Kenneth Lee Hodge. He told what happened in his statement to police. Kenneth Lee Hodge killed Harry Minds and took his billfold."

County Attorney Kenneth Sacks told the jury, "The investigation showed that Kenneth Lee Hodge murdered and robbed Harry Minds."

At the conclusion of Hodge's trial Judge R. Kent Martin read twenty-seven pages of instructions to the jury. Among the instructions were five choices the jury had for the verdict: guilty of first degree murder with the death penalty; guilty of first degree murder with life imprisonment; guilty of second degree murder with the penalty to be fixed by the court; not guilty by reason of insanity; and not guilty.

The jury's verdict came back after several ballots and ten hours of deliberation: Kenneth Lee Hodge was found guilty of first degree murder with recommended life imprisonment in the Iowa State Penitentiary. The defense attorney motioned for a new trial, but this was overruled by the judge. Hodge complained that he didn't feel as if he got a fair trial and that the jury was supposed to be twelve honest men and women. His appeals were denied.

LESSER CRIMINALS

The Council Bluffs Nonpareil newspapers relate any number of incidents that landed a person in the Pottawattamie County Jail for a few days up to six months. Many of the charges were for drunkenness, disturbing the peace, forgery or theft.

Frank "Monk" Trummer, an ex-convict and lecturer on 'Crime Does Not Pay' waived extradition to be taken to Auburn, Nebraska on a charge of arson in May of 1937. He was placed in the Pottawattamie County Jail before a deputy sheriff of Lincoln transported him to Auburn, Nebraska.

Brady Boone, age forty-nine was given fifteen days in the county jail on a charge of drunkenness December 30, 1915. Grace Lindsey a waitress in a Lower Broadway restaurant testified that he addressed her using insulting remarks.

H. R. Ames, age sixty-seven, was sentenced to ten days in jail for drunkenness.

Frank Gelser, age fifty-five, came into the warden's office on a Wednesday evening in 1915 and told the sergeant that he was under the influence of liquor and requested that he be locked up. He was accommodated.

Casper Kramer was charged with theft of an automobile on August 19, 1937. The auto belonged to Joe Rosenfeld of 420 South 8th Street in Council Bluffs. Kramer stole the car at 34th and Broadway. He was given a ten-month sentence and a $1,000 fine.

Michael E. Perrino, age thirty-four, living at 2800 Twin City Drive was held in the County Jail in 1937 for extradition to Medford, Oregon. Deputy sheriffs had made a routine check with the National Crime Information Center regarding a vehicle parked in front of Perrino's home. The report came back that he was wanted in Medford, Oregon on a check charge.

Larry E. Sprall, age twenty, of 23 Helen Avenue in Council Bluffs, was convicted of manslaughter for killing Arthur R. Warren, age twenty-four, a resident of Glenwood. While awaiting trial, on April 18, Sprall was released from the County Jail under bond. He had been held in the jail since February 10. Unable to post the required 10% of his original bond of $15,000, his attorneys Peter J. Peters and James A. Campbell petitioned Judge Leroy H. Johnson for a lowered bond. The Judge agreed and set the new bond at $2,500. Sprall's brother-in-law George Markey posted the $250.

December 6, 1937 found Frank Belt of 1608 South 13th Street in the county jail. He was found guilty of operating a motor vehicle while intoxicated. He was given ninety days and a fine of $300 and costs. One may wonder if he is related to Mike Belt, for still seen on the ceiling of one of the common areas is his name written in carbon smudge.

LaVerne Long, age seventeen, of 2135 Avenue A, committed a series of robberies over a three-month period of time. He was charged with breaking and entering the Crystal Ice Cream Company located at 2608 West Broadway with the intent to commit larceny. A motion to move the trial to juvenile court was denied because Long had recently served several months in the Training School for Boys in Eldora, Iowa. On December 23, 1939 he was found guilty and sentenced to a stint in the County Jail.

Blaine Lee, age twenty, of 808 ½ Broadway, served three days in the County Jail for petty larceny. He stole an iron radiator and iron boiler from Liberty Cleaners.

Jesse A. Mason, age thirty-six, was one of several named in indictments on July 27, 1939 for his alleged connection with making false insurance claims. He was arrested in a shack near the Missouri River four miles west of Honey Creek. He had been living in the shack all summer. He was arrested and placed in the Pottawattamie County Jail pending his hearing. He was indicted for fraudulent use of the mails involving false claims on insurance companies for alleged injuries in auto accidents.

September 13, 1939 Otto Carmichael of 1129 8th Avenue was given seven days in the County Jail for reckless driving and an auto collision where three persons were injured.

1969 was the last year the Pottawattamie County Jail was in use. At the end of the year it was closed, primarily for sanitation reasons. The following are some of the prisoners and their crimes from that last year.

Joseph A. Ryba, age twenty-nine, of 2820 Avenue C, was given a bond of $1,000 on an assault charge with intent to commit a felony. Ryba attempted to abduct a three-year-old girl. A report of this attempted abduction was called in to police and Ryba was arrested at the Riverside Apartments at 35th Street and 1st Avenue.

Charles LeManion, age twenty-six, also known as Charles M. Wagner was arrested at 9th Street and Avenue D. He was charged with receiving stolen property and carrying a concealed weapon. He pled innocent to both charges.

Daniel Hollins, age twenty of Omaha, and Ralph Richard Quinn, age eighteen of 1324 Avenue B, came into the warden's office of the Pottawattamie County Jail with a large bag of potato chips in late April of 1969. They said, "Give these to the boys in the back room," handed over the bag and left. Jailer Jess Poor noticed that the bag looked as if it had been opened. Within it he found two hack-saw blades. Hollins and Quinn were indicted and charged with attempting to assist prisoners to escape.

Clifford Earl Drumheller, age twenty, living at 1120 4th Avenue accumulated a number of charges by May of 1969, including breaking and entering on April 4, at Passer's Grocery Store at 2120 South 9th. He was arrested on the South Omaha Bridge on a drunk driving charge and for tampering with a motor vehicle. Drumheller tossed a beer can out of his car window and struck the windshield of another car, driven by Vernon Barnes. Drumheller was also charged for having no driver's license and resisting arrest. He was given thirty days in the Pottawattamie County Jail.

RICHARD WILSON

Richard Wilson, also known as Paul Wilson but most famously known as the Pennsylvania Kid, can claim the record for number of arrests and nights spent in the Pottawattamie County Jail over the years. Wilson was a hobo - one of many who traveled across the nation riding freight trains sometimes in box-cars, between cars or even on top of the train car, though riding atop any freight car was extremely dangerous. Wilson loved to ride just back of the brakeman.

Richard Wilson was a hobo that spent many a night in the Pottawattamie County Jail between 1931 and 1967. He was fingerprinted ninety-two times and claimed to be the dirtiest hobo in the nation.

In the 1930's it was estimated that there was a population of some two million hobos in the United States. Mostly men, they traveled about never staying in one place for very long. They would spend the night in hobo camps also called 'jungles' usually located near the railroad tracks. Often, they would do odd jobs to earn some money or even work in exchange for a meal or two. They had a code of ethics and even a secret sign language of markings that would inform other travelers of a friendly place to get a free meal or a little work. Wilson would often do some construction work to earn some money.

Richard Wilson was born around 1908 in Franklin, Pennsylvania. His father deserted his mother and his four siblings, and he was sent to foster care. He and his siblings were separated at the time of entering the foster care system, and he lost track of them. Towards the end of her life, though, he did visit his mother in a nursing home from time to time. He was born with club feet and was given an operation to correct the problem while in the foster system. He attended school through the eighth grade then left since he didn't care much for the folks that raised him. In the 1920's he began to ride the rails. His travels took him to all the contiguous United States, and even to Canada and Mexico. He often found himself in Council Bluffs as it was a hub for the railroad lines.

Between 1931-1967 Wilson was in the Squirrel Cage Jail arrested on multiple charges of vagrancy and illegal train riding. He was fingerprinted ninety-two times. He loved to make the claim that he was the dirtiest hobo in America. At one point when he was in the Pottawattamie County Jail, a deputy sheriff went with him to the bank to pay the rent for his safety deposit box. The deputy recounted to the Omaha World Herald newspaper in an interview with David Hading in July 2007, that Wilson was a bum who wasn't a bum. And that he smelled okay.

Wilson enjoyed his life as a hobo and made sure to attend the annual National Hobo Convention held in Britt, Iowa every August. Between 1963 and 1971 he was elected four times as the Hobo King.

The June 15, 1989 the Council Bluffs Nonpareil reported that Mr. Wilson, the Pennsylvania Kid, had died at the age of eighty-three. He had been unwell for the last twelve years of his life and instead of sleeping under bridges and in box-cars he had been living at the Tabor Manor Care Center in Tabor, Iowa. His body was cremated, and his ashes were scattered along the tracks by "Iowa Blackey" one of his hobo friends. A fitting end for a man who spent his life riding the rails.

WOMEN PRISONERS

Women housed in the front section of the second floor were incarcerated for many of the same crimes as the male prisoners. At times, the children of these women were also housed in the women's detention cells as they had no other place to go while their mothers were locked up. Crimes of forgery, drunk and disorderly, disturbing the peace, prostitution and even violent crime were quite commonly listed in the prison records as the reasons for incarceration. The Council Bluffs Nonpareil newspaper published the crimes as well as the punishment for the women, as they did for the men. These women prisoners were housed separately from the men on the second floor of the jail. Some of them could be tough gals. Marie Maxine Spengler was one such woman.

MARIE MAXINE SPANGLER

In the last days of December of 1925, she was caught forging checks. In Des Moines the forgeries added up to $300 and an undisclosed amount from four Council Bluffs businesses. She often used the alias of Avis Archer and gave her address as 1502 10th Avenue in Council Bluffs. She put on a tough façade for one so young. Standing before the judge she was asked if she wished to waive preliminary hearing of her case and also waive the grand jury, as she previously intimated to the county attorney. She placed her finger in her mouth, giggled and with a tilt of her head simpered a 'yes' to the judge. She displayed the actions of a ten-year-old, recorded the judge. Though a juvenile, she was tried as an adult because at sixteen she was married to Mr. Frank Spangler.

"I'm glad to go to the pen, just to get out of this hick town," declared Marie Maxine Spangler as she was sentenced to ten years at the women's reformatory for forging checks and cashing them with Council Bluffs merchants. Merchants reported that they were disarmed by her engaging smile and light-hearted conversation as she passed bad and forged checks without batting an eye.

Marie Maxine Spengler was tried for forgery and passing bad checks to merchants in Des Moines and Council Bluffs. During her trial she put on a tough-girl façade telling the judge that she was sick of this hick town and glad to go to the pen. She was photographed reading a true confessions magazine and smoking.

As she left the court, she clutched her husband, Frank Spengler in a close embrace and said: "You won' forget to send your baby plenty of cigarettes, will you?" Marie smoked almost constantly.

While housed at the county jail some of her school friends came by to see her. For once she shattered the hardened girl-prisoner façade and broke down and cried pitifully over what had happened and what was to come. She admonished her friends not to start smoking and not to run with a rough crowd.

Sheriff Lainson and his wife accompanied Marie Spangler to Rockwell City to begin her term. In the photo she sits waiting to be transported to the women's reformatory, smoking and reading a true confessions magazine.

OTHER WOMEN PRISONERS

Josephine Spolar, age twenty-nine, resided at 631 South 19th in Omaha. She and her roommate and friend Hazel Flahart, age twenty-six, partied a little too much in a Council Bluffs bar in early September of 1939. The women were charged with intoxication, resisting an officer, using obscene language and disturbing the peace. It was reported that Flahart used the worst kind of language when confronted. She threw a high-heeled shoe at the officer hitting him in the shoulder and kicked him in the groin when he took her into custody. Spolar pled guilty, Flahart pled not-guilty. When Flahart could offer no defense, she was judged guilty. Both women were sentenced to thirty days in the Pottawattamie County Jail.

On Thanksgiving Day of 1937 Mrs. Jessie Mitchner, age forty-six, residing at 2311 South 6th Street in Council Bluffs, was arrested for disturbing the peace. On that day she was charged with yelling profane names at Billy Masters, age ten, and his playmate in the backyard of Mr. and

Mrs. Divine of 2309 South 6th Street. She denied doing so. The two boys testified and shocked the courtroom as they related their experiences. She was found guilty and received thirty days.

In that same year, Martha Klots, proprietor of the Silver Dollar Club and Mary Potkonjak a waitress at the club, were given fifteen days in the county jail for selling beer to a minor at the club.

Margaret Reed, age forty-three, a housewife who lived at 1513 South Main Street in Council Bluffs found herself in jail again. She had previously served two days for drunkenness. Intoxicated once again she was given a similar sentence. In her defense she stated her situation. "I intended to go to my sister's home near Manawa, but somehow I never got there."

The Squirrel Cage Jail sits behind the courthouse on a snowy afternoon in the 1920's.

JUVENILE DETENTION

The area of women's detention was also used to house juvenile prisoners, or even the children of an incarcerated adult if no other shelter could be found for them. Mothers were often left with the choice of bringing their children to the jail with them or leaving them to fend for themselves on the streets. There were no child services to take the children in those days. The officials at the jail worked with a Christian children's home in the area to find other housing.

Early on, juveniles housed in the jail were between ages three and thirteen years. Later, children between ages seven and seventeen were housed in this area. Their crimes would vary from theft and vandalism, but most commonly these children were runaways or had been caught in possession of adult beverages.

JAIL BREAKS

One thing all prisons have in common are attempted jail breaks by those incarcerated within their walls. The Pottawattamie County Jail has had its fair share of attempts. Each time after an escape, be it successful or thwarted in the plan, changes were made to the jail, the housing of prisoners or policies as a result of these daring attempts. A few of these incidents are related here.

From time to time improvements were made in the hopes to deter prisoners from attempting to break out of jail, or to have them easily recognized if they did escape. In July of 1914 workmen began to remove the old wire at the Pottawattamie County Jail. A new steel burglar-proof barrier around the building was to be installed, hopefully rendering the jail impervious to assault from without or escape from within on the part of the prisoners. This new fence was to be eight feet high, with steel posts set in concrete with sharpened steel spikes, placed so that they could not be scaled.

In April of 1914 the roof needed more attention. Workmen removed the old tar and gravel roof from both the jail and courthouse and a new rubberoid sheath was installed; this would then be covered with asphalt and gravel.

December 5, 1888 only three years after the jail was built, eleven bold prisoners managed to walk out of the jail. They left unnoticed, using the front door, much to the chagrin of County Sheriff James O'Neill.

About 4 o'clock in the afternoon the eleven prisoners walked out the front door of the Pottawattamie County Jail without any interference, all except the last man to leave the building. The prisoner Mulligan was a little slower than the rest of the departing guests of the county. He was collared by the nephew of Mrs. O'Neill, the sheriff's wife. Young Mr. Hallman was returning from the courthouse. Approaching the jail, Hallman recognized Mulligan as an inmate and tackled him. After a brief tussle he managed to get the prisoner back inside the jail.

After a quick inspection of the cells, word was sent immediately to Sheriff O'Neil, who was still at the courthouse, that ten other prisoners were missing from the jail. The escaped prisoners were listed as Leonard, Woods, Shoemaker, Sullivan, Aull, Raymond, Reynolds, Ferguson, Diamond and Mulligan. Though Mulligan had been apprehended immediately.

A manhunt began right away. It didn't take long for two of the escapees to be located at the Driving Park. Johnson and Diamond were running away. Officers quickly overtook the men. Diamond had just been sentenced on the previous Saturday to serve four years for the burglary of the Crippen Store in Neola.

Another prisoner, Aull was caught shortly after the capture of Johnson and Diamond. The rest remained at large. Telegrams were sent to other law enforcement agencies alerting them of the escaped prisoners.

An inspection of the jail took place to ascertain how the prisoners had escaped. Prisoners had secured a file somehow and cut the lock on the door leading from the exercise corridor to the court or back corridor, which encircles the part of the jail consisting of the large cylinder of cells. Once into the court it was easy for the men to climb the grating that extends from the first floor to the third floor of the building. No prisoners had been housed on the third floor for some time and the sheriff had left those doors unlocked. How the prisoners learned of this is not known. Whether they overheard a conversation, or it was discovered accidently, it assisted their plan of escape.

The men got past the grating on the third level and passed through the upper front corridor, then down two flights of stairs and out the front door of the jail. The men had to pass by the doors of the sheriff's household apartments on the first floor, but they would not have been discovered if Hallman hadn't happened to encounter Mulligan leaving.

Closer inspection of the lock revealed that preparations for the escape had been in place for some time. Traces of filings were discovered on the floor by where the hasp of the lock was filed through, the final 1/16th of an inch finished that day. The sheriff claimed that there had been two locks and two sets of chains in place before the escape. However, no sign of the second lock or any chains were discovered upon the inspection.

In 1914 Sheriff Hazen discovered some prisoners attempting to escape. Three men decamped having sawn through the bars of a window and let themselves down the outside of the building using a rope of blankets. The men did not get far. In October of 1915 the sheriff decided that all prisoners would wear carpet slippers and be deprived of individual clothing. Jumper suits were issued. He was hopeful this would deter any further escapes, such as the attempt in the previous year.

In 1935 John Fador who was being held in connection with the shooting of a watchman in Missouri Valley, Iowa, broke a fixture off a radiator to use as a weapon in an attempt to escape. Jailer Howard, acting on a tip he received from a trusty took the weapon from Fador, thwarting his escape attempt.

On April 28, 1937 another group of prisoners sawed their way out of the Pottawattamie County Jail. As soon as the break was noticed the remaining twenty-four prisoners were turned out of their cells and into the bullpen. This was discovered at 7:00 A. M. on Monday. There they remained all day until their evening meal. Every night the routine of night check began at 7:00 P. M. and continued to 7:30 P. M. as prisoners were transferred to their cells for the night. It was estimated that the escape took place between 7:00 and 7:30 in the previous evening.

When questioned after being captured and returned to the jail, James Kennedy said that he found a broken saw in the bullpen and began to saw at the bars. He refused to tell authorities where he'd gotten the saw blade. Kennedy and Howard Wolford took turns sawing at the iron bars. They managed to get three bars sawed off and got into the windows of the west side of the common area. Kennedy then opened the heavy screen wire ventilator and held it open as the other seven men crawled through. The men then dropped four feet to the ground, scaled the eight-foot fence in the jail yard and each of the men went in pairs in separate directions.

Window through which many saws entered to assist in jail breaks. On first floor bullpen area a window located on the first floor of the Pottawattamie County Jail in the bullpen area once had ventilation grating to prevent escape. Those aiding prisoners in escape would toss saw blades into the ventilator and prisoners would fish them out and begin sawing at the bars, and even the ventilators themselves.

Authorities believed that the saws got into the jail by way of that same ventilator. They found a tin can jammed into where it had been pried open for the escape. The sheriff said it was impossible to get the ventilator open from the inside, that someone had done this to assist in getting the prisoners out of the jail.

When asked about how long it took them to saw through the iron bars, the prisoner, Kennedy laughed and said they would be surprised how easy it was to get through the bars. They sawed them half way off then broke them. The opening measured 15-½ inches by 11-½ inches. No one heard the sawing because a radio in the jailer's quarters masked the sounds of sawing.

As soon as could be managed an iron plate was welded into place.

The Council Bluffs Nonpareil listed the names, ages, addresses and crimes of the escaped prisoners. Meril Roy, age twenty, of 700 4th Street, one year for forgery; Virgil Montgomery, age twenty-three, of 815 Avenue E, one year for receiving stolen property; James Francis Kennedy, age twenty-three, of 417 E. Washington Avenue, one year for forgery; Warren Jones, age eighteen of 1513 5th Avenue; Howard Wolford, age twenty-four, of 1314 W. Broadway, one year for forgery; Jack Rhoades, age twenty-two, of 1611 Avenue M, one year for receiving stolen property; Clyde Wolford, age twenty-seven and brother of Howard Wolford, also residing at 1317 W. Broadway, one year for forgery. Floyd Poyer, age twenty-two, of 14th and Broadway, was awaiting trial for auto theft.

Some of the men were apprehended quickly. Three of the men were back in custody the next day while five remained at large. James Francis Kennedy was picked up at the Illinois Central round house. He had first walked to the river then back to the roundhouse. Warren Jones who was serving a one-year sentence for burglary was picked up at 10:00 P. M.

at a beer tavern at 19th Street and Broadway. Howard Wolford was soon after caught in Sioux City, Iowa.

June 9, 1937, seven of eight prisoners who sawed their way out of the county jail on April 28 were back in custody and pled guilty to jailbreaking. Judge John P. Tinley sentenced the men to one year at the reformatory at Anamosa Iowa. These men were already serving sentences for other crimes when they escaped.

The eighth prisoner, Floyd Poyner still remained at large.

THE OLD JAIL, to which two deputies are taking a young man, is more picturesque tha efficient. Dating from 1880, it lacks many of the facilities a modern jail should have.

Deputies take a prisoner to jail. Some prisoners claimed that they would prefer to serve a longer sentence in any other jail.

Dick Harrison also escaped the jail in that same year. On July 25, 1937 Dick Harrison, a trusty of the Pottawattamie County Jail was captured at his home at Lake Manawa after authorities got a tip. When they entered the home, they found Harrison hiding under the bed. One month previously Harrison had escaped from jail where he was serving a ninety-day sentence on an illegal liquor charge. He had served half his term when he escaped.

An attempted jailbreak was thwarted on Sunday evening May 29, 1939 by Sheriff Riley C. Nelson and his staff of deputies. Three prisoners were involved. A tip had been given to the sheriff about the possibility of a jail break being planned, so a watch was maintained for two weeks. Having learned that the ringleader of the jail break was Louis Axtell, the sheriff had him removed and transferred to Fort Madison on Saturday, instead of Monday, ahead of his scheduled transfer date. Axtell was serving a five-year sentence for the theft of a heifer.

The sharp eyes of Paul Johnson, the twelve-year-old son of Bastin Johnson, the jailer, led to the discovery. Paul was visiting his father and playing on the lawn. About 7:20 P M he noticed two arms moving back and forth on the bars of the west window of the jail.

"What is that man rubbing back and forth on the bars for?" Paul asked his father. Immediately the jailer alerted Sheriff Nelson who got assistance from five policemen. The men concealed themselves around the jail, expecting the escape to take place between 7:30 and 7:45 P. M. when the inmates were taken out of the bullpen and locked in their separate cells for the night. Two bars had been cut from a bullpen window on the west side of the jail near the window where eight men had escaped two years earlier.

Officers heard the thump of an iron bar falling, then another thump. Then an arm reached out the window trying to bend down the ventilator screen. Unable to bend it, as the prisoner had not cut enough of the wire, officers closed in on them arresting the two men attempting to escape: Kenneth Hannan who was being held on forgery charges and Jack

Stevens, alias Inman, serving one year for forgery. Hannan and Stevens were taken and strip-searched looking for weapons and saws.

An investigation followed. The two iron bars that had been sawed were located under the turn-table that operated the revolving cells. It was discovered that about ten saw blades had been thrown over the jail picket fence and landed atop the screen window ventilator. Axtell had fished them out through the window and had set to work sawing for about ten days. He would fill in the cuts he made to the bars with paper and soap. As soon as a blade was worn down it was broken up and tossed out of the window and into the alley on the north side of the jail. Stevens told authorities that Axtell left two remaining blades behind when he was transferred so Stevens and Hannan could finish the job.

A mangled lock on a cell that was broken in an escape.

A light snow was falling in the early hours of Christmas day of 1945. A trusty of the Pottawattamie County Jail, Carl Edward Johnson took the iron bars, he had been secretly sawing, from the window without waking his fellow trusty, Bernard F. Smith, and slipped from the basement of the jail unnoticed. Emerging on the east side of the jail he walked away, down the drive and into the silence of the falling snow. At 7:00 A. M. on Tuesday morning when jailor Jim Johnson unlocked the door to the trusty cell located in the basement of the Squirrel Cage Jail to release Johnson and Smith for their duties assisting in the kitchen for meal preparation for all inmates, only Bernard Smith still slumbered in his cot.

The trusty sleeping quarters were located in the basement below the dining area of the main jail. A heavily barred window on the east side of the jail provided some light and air to this room. The jailor saw that three bars in a segment of the iron grill had been removed allowing for a small opening just big enough for a small man to squeeze through.

Christmas Day in 1945 Carl Edward Johnson escaped from his basement cell where he was housed as a trusty. He had sawed through three of the bars and wriggled through the gap, walking off in the evening as a light snow was falling in the evening. The sheriff looks out from the bars of Johnson's escape route.

Monday night at 8:00 P. M. the two trusties had been securely locked into their quarters. When questioned about Carl Johnson sawing at the bars, his trusty cell mate Smith said he had not seen or heard anything. Neither did he see Johnson leave. Sheriff Jack Taylor believed that Johnson must have sawed through the bars in the daytime hours unnoticed. Trusties were given freedom to move about within the jail while carrying out their duties, unlike other prisoners who were confined to their cells or the common recreational areas. Johnson had been arrested six weeks earlier on a charge of taking an automobile without permission. He admitted to being intoxicated at the time. His sentence was six months.

Carl Edward Johnson was tracked to Santa Cruz, California where he had been arrested for forgery and was incarcerated.

After this jail break the bars in the basement were removed and the windows bricked over. Other entry ways to the basement were covered over as well. The basement was no longer used except for the boiler, which had been added to provide central heating.

A metal plate was welded to the iron bars as a temporary fix after Johnson's escape. Later, the bars were removed and left on the basement floor. The windows were bricked in, and the room used to house trusties was moved to the third floor. The bars are still lying on the floor of the basement just where repairmen left them in 1945.

In both 1958 and 1962 Mr. Barrett was incarcerated in the Pottawattamie County Jail. Two times he managed to escape by way of the toilet unit in his cell that went into the core in the center of the rotary mechanism. He climbed up to the top of the sanitation and sewerage core, pushed back the heavy, wedge-shaped iron grate atop the core and came out of the central area at the forth floor. This was the residence area of the warden or jailer for the prison. When he peeked out of the door that gives access to the core area he was greeted, both times by the jailer, happy to assist him back into his cell.

Mr. Barrett tried to escape twice using the same escape route both times. During his stay at the jail in both 1958 and 1962, he attempted to climb up the inner core of the toilets and emerge on the forth floor pushing up the hatch and entering the residential area of the warden. Bill Foster was warden then and had opted to live in another area of the jail, so those rooms were not used. Barrett failed to escape each time.

October 12, 1964 John H. Croghan, age twenty-eight of Crescent, Iowa, fought his way out of the jail at about 5:30 in the evening. He had been arrested January 2, 1964 for breaking and entering the Johnson Pharmacy and was serving his sentence when he escaped. Jailer William Foster, age fifty-eight, was returning a prisoner to the third-floor lock-up and unlocked the door. Croghan, housed on the third floor as well, rushed out and tried to push past Foster. The two men fought all the way down the metal stairway. A trusty who had been helping in the kitchen joined in the fight to try and subdue Croghan. Croghan broke free, losing his shoes in the melee, rushed out the kitchen door in his stocking feet and disappeared through the alley by the jail. Dogs led officers down nearby 6th Street and 5th Avenue but lost the trail between some garages.

When he was recaptured a few days later he stated that he had nothing against the jail staff. "They treated me pretty good." His greatest complaint about the jail was that it was "not fit for dogs."

October 25, 1966 two prisoners sawed their way out of the County Jail. William Foster, the jailer, discovered the men missing about 7:45 A. M. when he delivered breakfast to the prisoners. Milo Alexander Constandine, age forty-four, was being held on charges of attempting to break and enter, and Roger William Steele, age thirty, from Pipestone Minnesota, was awaiting sentencing for a breaking and entering charge. It was believed that the men escaped about 9:30 the previous evening after Foster had given the prisoners supper about 6:20 that night. The men used an eighteen-inch-long steel bar broken off of a mesh window covering of a window in the bullpen of the jail. They used the steel bar to break the lock of the barred door, then cut through the ½ inch steel hasp of the padlocked outside door. They went down the fire escape on the south side of the building, down the stairs into the jail yard and over the fence.

The saw blades were not found. Another prisoner in jail on an embezzlement charge declined to join the two men making their escape.

June 25, 1969 Curtis D. Evans, age twenty-three of 2732 Avenue L was held in the jail in lieu of a $1,000 bond on a charge of escaping from Mercy Hospital a week before, after he had been taken there for treatment. He was caught fourteen minutes later.

January 1, 1969 has the most unique events in a jail break. Michael Lee Rhoades, age eighteen, of 22 N. 15th Street managed to dig through the first-floor wall of the common room with a steel leg from a table. He broke through the steel plate and brickwork and around 10:30 that night he crawled through the hole he'd made into the yard, climbed over the fence and fled. With him also went William Lee Jorgensen, age twenty-five, of 502 4th Street, who was serving a one-year sentence with a fine of $24 for breaking and entering, and three years for a conspiracy charge connected to the break-in. Michael Frederick Pond, age nineteen, of 2605 3rd serving a sentence for larceny theft of a motor vehicle and parole violation and Ralph Wayne Taylor, age thirty-nine, of Kansas City, Kansas, also accompanied the fleeing prisoners. Seven others incarcerated in the jail refused to join the escapees. The men were all back in custody by the next day. Michael Frederick Pond turned himself in the next day; the other three were caught and returned to their cells.

The unique part of this escape was a note left behind by one of the men. The note was written on some cardboard clipped from a Monopoly game box and had the word "Unshackled" torn from a magazine pasted above the note. The note read as follows, "Dear Sir, I sincerely hope that this escape will help you get a new jail because you need one. I knot [knocked] out the wall in an hour. Sincerely youers, Mike and Bill K. C."

No one heard any unusual noises while the wall was being breached. No one would say who the prisoner was that dug through the wall, except that he labored for five days. He let water out of the radiator causing it to knock. Each time the radiator made the knocking noise he would hit the wall. During times he was not digging, the wall was covered with newspaper.

The County Board of Supervisors ordered the welding of a metal plate over the hole and replacement of the bricks.

Upon their escape, the four men went to Rhoades' house where he went in alone and asked his father, Leo, to drive him to Omaha, His father refused, and said he was going to drive him back to the jail. When Leo Rhoades got in the car the other three men were waiting for him. They forced Leo to drive them to Omaha. When the men got out, Leo called the sheriff's office at 11:00 P. M. to report the escape. Soon after all four men were taken into custody and returned to the jail.

GRAFITTI

Over the centuries people have left their mark upon places of incarceration carved in the walls of their cells. The Squirrel Cage Jail inmates were no different. Each cell has its own unique collection of words and pictures etched into the thick layers of gray paint.

Often the prisoners in the hold-over cells would write their names, their charges and days spent in the jail. One man carved the menu of the fair offered each day. On alternating days, oatmeal or Cream of Wheat for breakfast. Dinner would vary from soup and chicken to noodles and wieners, with meat and potatoes on Sunday. For supper eggs, sandwiches, beans, potatoes and spaghetti were served. According to the newspapers, on Christmas in 1939 prisoners of the Squirrel Cage Jail were traditionally treated to a special dinner by Bastin Johnson the jailer. Each prisoner was served roast chicken, cranberry sauce, celery, green beans, bread and coffee with a dessert of mince pie.

Time in jail passes slowly. Prisoners would count the days until their release. Many made a calendar was drawn on the prison walls of their cells to mark time.

Another found in the maximum-security section reads "Rin Tin Tin rusted to death here in 1960." The third floor where the men were incarcerated for more severe crimes has the most colorful graffiti such as a naked woman, rude words to the jailer Bill Foster and his wife, of faces, eyes watching, 'The End' and someone with a good sense of humor drew a doorbell on their cell asking for people to ring the doorbell. Over the years graffiti was painted over and lost, yet as the paint peels off the old walls, haunting images emerge.

At times, the prisoners showed a sense of humor about their time in jail. One prisoner installed a pencil drawing of a doorbell on his cell door.

Doodling and writing on the bars passed the rime. One prisoner wrote a rude message to the jailer, Bill Foster and his wife.

An inmate carved a drawing of a sexy woman with a guitar while Doug Lantry counted down the days of his jail sentence in his cell.

Another prisoner left behind a pencil drawing of a reclining woman. The image had been painted over, yet it erodes from the peeling paint like a spectral memory. A prisoner lying in the bunk would see her face next to his, recumbent beside him.

Sometimes the men would paste letters cut from magazines to express themselves. One such example read: "Turn onto Jail. Life, it's a downer." None of these survived, and neither did any photographs of them.

One graffiti artist remembered, with humor, a jail break attempt. One of the prisoners was burrowing his way through the wall and got to within fourteen inches before he was caught. After repairs were made someone wrote on the spot, "Exit Only."

The table in the common room or bullpen was also an easy target for prison house graffiti. Tim Fipps, Tim Johnson, names carved over previous ones, weaves a tale of so many incarcerated in the jail.

In the bullpen there was little to pass the time other than read, play monopoly, cards or carve their names into the wooden table.

Graffiti is also on the ceilings of the men's cell recreational area. These were smudged in carbon from burning ends of paper rolled tightly which were used to write upon the ceiling. One man attempting to write up there fell to his death near the end of the solitary hallway.

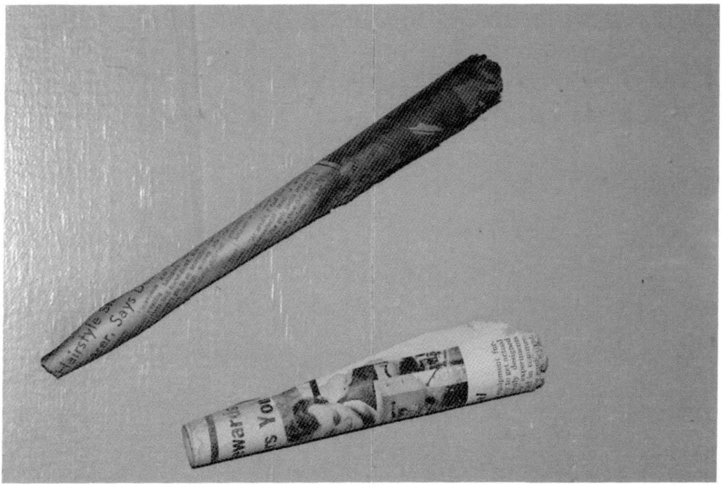

Other forms of graffiti that the prisoners would leave behind were to write their names on the ceilings using smudge sticks of rolled up paper set on fire. The carbon from the burning paper would be their ink to use in writing.

Where a prisoner could reach, he would create the carbon writing on ceiling with the home-made smudge sticks.

The women's section has a number of Biblical inscriptions and on one of the bunks someone painstakingly carved a checkers board to help pass the time in play.

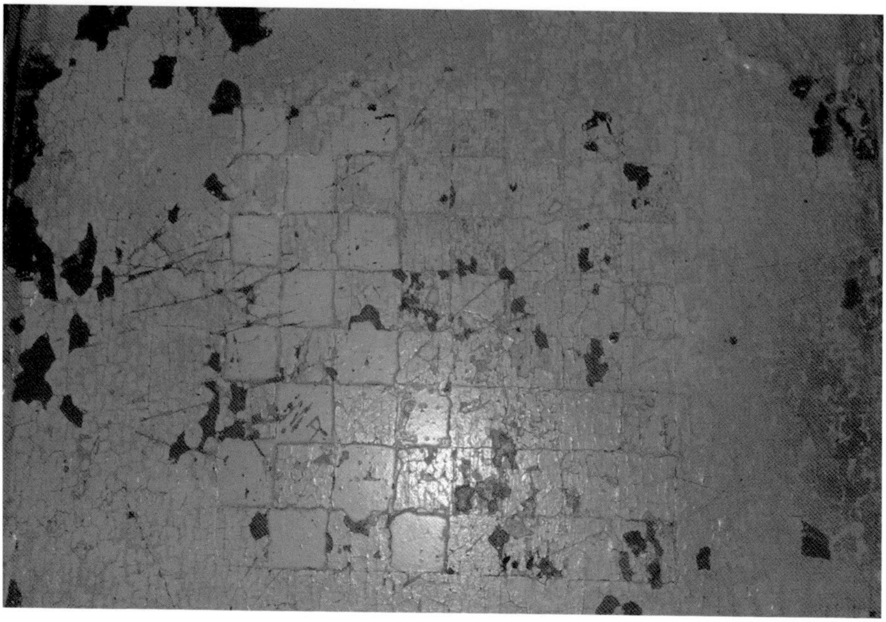

A prisoner carved a checkerboard into the layers of paint on a top bunk in a women's detention cell.

THE END OF THE LINE

The jail, in its day, was a modern and radical marvel in penal architecture. It was erected in 1885 with a promise of ease of operation for the warden and security of housing prisoners with low possibilities of escape. However, by 1887 there were already issues with the three-story rotary structure. Sanitary, structural and mechanical problems quickly arose. These same issues would continue to plague the jail for years. These problems were not unique to the Pottawattamie County "Squirrel Cage" Jail.

Over the years the jail changed but little. Though the landscaping varied, the jail remained almost unchanged since it was built in 1885. Plumbing, electrical and heating systems were installed over the years.

The three-story Pottawattamie County Jail was the largest rotary jail constructed of the eighteen jails of this design which were built across the Midwest in the 1880's. Currently, only three of these unique rotary jails are still standing and all have been converted into museums. A single-story jail is located in Gallatin, Missouri and a two-story jail is located in Crawfordsville, Indiana. The three-story rotary jail is in Council Bluffs.

Trouble for these rotary jails began within two years after construction. The giant rotary jail proved to be unsatisfactory because the inner drum failed "to scour." March 18, 1887 the *Globe* reported on the issues plaguing the jail.

> *The fact need not be concealed that the new county jail is pretty near a failure. The great revolving cylinder which contains most of the cells in the building does not work on its axis with satisfaction. It is thought by some of our officials that although this drum may be made to work for quite a while yet-possibly for years-it is a failure. It is not exactly in harmony with the building nor with itself. The time may come when it will be taken out, for it cannot be used as a stationary apartment of cells. It is so large and heavy that it does not sit gracefully on its foundation. In fact, it don't scour. If it should be taken down and apart, and removed from the jail, we would still have a jail left though not a very serviceable one. It is rumored that the revolving jail at Maryville is working badly-also that some prisoners have escaped therefrom. It would be a difficult task for a mechanic to reconstruct our jail and supply it with stationary cells-yet it could of course be done. New things are dreadfully uncertain, like most old ones. It is possible that there may be a poor, wise man somewhere in Council Bluffs who has time to revolve this cylinder in his mind until he can tell what to do with it-if not we will have to refer it to a Philadelphia lawyer, knowing that what he don't know is beyond human wit.*

The county jail in Maryville, Nodaway County, Missouri, soon developed mechanical difficulties in the rotary cylinder. Not long after the completion of the jail certain mechanical difficulties developed in the gears making it difficult to rotate the inner cylinder. Nodaway County Sheriff Earl M. Brown reported at the time of the inspection that the unit had failed 'to scour' and that on certain occasions the prisoners 'rocked' the inner cylinder making it impossible to revolve the huge cylinder. In 1904 a prisoner, Charles Fry, was killed when his head was crushed between the inner and outer grids while the cylinder was being revolved.

From about 1910, grand juries began to complain about conditions at these jails. Fire marshals also registered fire hazard objections. Because the rotary mechanism in the Maryville, Missouri jail failed, in 1938 the inner rotary cylinder was welded to the stationary outer shell. Doors were cut for each cell and a wide circular catwalk was erected at the second level for access to the cells. By 1957, Sheriff Remley had renovated the entire structure and modern plumbing and heating systems placed in the buildings. The look of the jail remained basically the same, except for the addition of the catwalk, but the problems and hazards related to the rotary mechanism had successfully been eliminated. At present the huge circular gridded cage remains within the large room. The sheriff indicated that various attempts had been made to raze the building, but without success.

The Daviess County Jail in Gallatin, Missouri, was built in 1888 by the B. Pauley Jail Building and Manufacturing Company of St. Louis, Missouri, after the design of the patentee, W. H. Brown. The entire cost of the jail and the sheriff's apartment amounted to $12,000. This jail is identical to the other rotary jails except for some minor changes in the locking device, the gear mechanism, and the fact that it has only one level or deck with eight cells. At the time of the inspection, Sheriff L. H. Houghton explained that the rotary mechanism was still usable, but in need of repairs. However, the county had so few prisoners that there was no need of more than one cell at a time and that was usually used for one solitary 'drunk' at the time. In the past, the county had been the scene of much local color: Frank James, the brother of Jesse James, was tried and acquitted in the old courthouse in Gallatin shortly after the Civil War.

Complaints about the rotary jails across the Midwest were common. During the labor troubles in Kansas in 1917, Ellen Reeve Bloor, a labor leader, described the Wichita jail when she visited some of the imprisoned laborers. "All were immediately arrested and locked up in the Wichita jail, one of the worst I have ever seen. The cells were angular cubicles, shaped like pie-cuts, rotating around a piston in the center, keeping the prisoners exposed through the grating and in continual motion. The guard was able to stand still and watch them as they moved. All sense of human dignity was murdered in that place. On my first visit there, one of the boys warned us, 'Don't stand near the walls anywhere, they are alive with bugs.' One of the men in that prison went insane. Another died. Though this form of jail was very secure against escape the great argument for its disuse was that it was a human firetrap."

In Pottawattamie County these same issues confronted officials. The jail received its first onslaught of major problems when, in 1908, the county grand jury called the crusty old clink a health hazard.

In August 27, 1937 five south-west Iowa jails were given a satisfactory rating by the federal prison inspector. In the written report given to county officials it was recommended that a drinking fountain be installed on the ground floor bullpen and to install auto flushers for the toilets in the cells. Authorities quickly contacted plumbers to make these changes and upgrades to the jail. The inspector Mr. Anderson commented, "your jail is in fine condition except that it is so old and antiquated."

Since 1943 the Pottawattamie County Jail was condemned by twenty-four different grand juries. In 1964 many district court judges refused to send prisoners to the Squirrel Cage Jail, utilizing alternative places to incarcerate prisoners. They even closed the jail for a six-month period because the conditions were so deplorable. In 1964 the County Board of Supervisors proposed a bond issue of $440,000 to build a new jail. This was overwhelmingly voted down.

Not only did the jail have issues with the rotary mechanism not functioning properly, prisoners were making attempts at breaking out. An earlier chapter deals with the escapes in more depth. Three years after the completion of the county jail, the Council Bluffs Nonpareil newspaper reported the events.

> *One of the boldest and most successful jail deliveries on record in the state occurred in this city at about 4 o'clock yesterday afternoon, when eleven prisoners cooly walked out the front door of the county jail and took their immediate departure without interference from anyone. The prisoners effected their escape by filing the lock on the door leading from the exercise room to the back corridor. From here they climbed up the grating of the outer shell to the third floor and walked out through an unlocked front door. As a result of the escape Sheriff O'Neill was criticized for 'grossest negligence'.*

Apart from the mechanical difficulties, the county jail proved hazardous for the prisoners. Almost without exception month after month prisoners received broken arms, legs, a foot or hand caught between the bars during the revolving of the cylinder. As the drum began to rotate the prisoner would purposefully put a limb out to be mangled in the hopes of getting time out of their little pie-shaped cell. This proved futile as a means of any lengthy escape from the confines of their cell as they would quickly be taken to the infirmary and the doctor would set the bone or tend to what was needed and, within hours, the prisoner was back in his cell.

Sanitation in the jail proved to be an ongoing and difficult matter to deal with. The prisoners would attempt to clog the toilet system. Trash and other detritus would litter their cells. Over the years the respective county sheriffs complained to county officials about the conditions, and various grand juries in their annual reports condemned the building time and time again. Efforts were made to clean up the persistent problems typical of any institution where men are housed under lock and key in tight quarters. These were temporary fixes to the overarching problems of the penal system and of this particular jail, for all too soon the jail become unfit once again for human habitation.

View of a cell in a county jail
Pottawattamie County "Squirrel Cage" Jail
1960

Unsanitary conditions were a constant problem in the jail. A 1960 photo reveals the living conditions of a prisoner.

Critics of the rotary jail would state that the accommodations did not take into account the welfare of the inmates in this design. However, compared to other jails of the day in Council Bluffs and other cities, the rotary jail came off as a palace compared to the gritty conditions and filth of the other local hoosegows. The battle for decent housing of prisoners continued for years.

In September of 1960 the Pottawattamie County Jail came under fire one more time, this time the five district court judges who inspected the jail ruled it must be vacated, citing sanitary and safety reasons for their decision. They stated that conditions were so deplorable that they refused to sentence law breakers to the inadequate Pottawattamie County Jail. The number of juvenile offenders that would have been incarcerated in the Squirrel Cage Jail in 1968 alone would have been 252 for larceny/theft, fifty-four for auto theft, sixty-eight for disorderly conduct, seventy-eight for drunkenness, sixty for burglary and thirty-four for vandalism.

With the rotation device disabled in 1960, the decline over the next decade culminated on December 1, 1969 when the state ruled the jail unfit to house prisoners. Only when the jail was closed in December 1969 did the issues become resolved for this jail, with the prisoners and problems transferred to another site of incarceration.

A new courthouse was being built to replace the old one that had developed structural issues. Within the new courthouse there would be a jail on the top floor. The question arose of what to do with the inadequate and antiquated Squirrel Cage Jail. Many wanted to tear it down, others fought to preserve it for its architectural uniqueness.

The old courthouse was slated for destruction. In 1972 it was discovered that the building was sinking at a rate of two inches a month. A committee reported that costs would have been prohibitive to repair the building, plus it was considered to be sadly out of date.

NEW LIFE

In 1969 a study was done looking into the costs to bring the Squirrel Cage Jail up to meet minimum standards for prisons in Iowa and the nation. A bond issue had recently failed that asked for about $450,000 to build a new facility. The estimated cost of $492,499 was only to repair the building, not any part of the jail facility. However, this plan would not bring the jail up to regulations to meet the minimum government specifications. Nor would it be able to meet Council Bluffs building codes. Another $7,470 would be needed to construct a new kitchen and wash room area. This would not include the cost of total demolition of the original facilities. The cost to replace and bring the electrical and mechanicals up to code would be another $29,000. No one wanted to invest that much money in the antiquated, dinosaur of a jail.

The unique Squirrel Cage Jail was on the chopping block and was scheduled to be torn down. Because of the unique design of this jail a movement began to preserve it for future generations. It was a battle that would rage on for over a decade before the fate of the jail was finally decided.

In late November of 1969, before the jail was closed, Charles Lessig, historical architect for the National Park Service in Washington DC, was named to serve on a committee to study the possibility of creating a museum out of the Squirrel Cage Jail. Along with Mr. Lessig, Bill Dean, assistant Director of the National Park Service, and Robert Giles of Omaha, regional Director for the National Parks Service, worked with Frederic Schlott, the president of the Council Bluffs Park Board, to seek the cooperation of the County Board of Supervisors in order to preserve this unique jail.

In contrast to the previous reports, these reports came back stating that the jail was in an excellent state of preservation. This particular rotary jail is the only three-story jail structure still standing in the nation, thus increasing the historical value of the building. Giles stated that this jail "exemplifies one of the most unique and ingeniously designed jails of its time in the country. The jail depicts a way of life of social institutions to cope with the troublesome days in certain parts of the Midwest where mob violence, lynchings and lawlessness prevailed." In this statement he is referring to the actions that terrified the nation by such notorious outlaws as Jesse James. The Park Board sought to preserve the old jail through the Historic Dodge House organization, scheduling meetings with the County Board of Supervisors to discuss preservation. At the time they believed that there were only three of these rotary jails built, and the one in Council Bluffs was the last of its kind still intact.

The kitchen looked in dire condition before restoration.

The walls were bare of plaster and a stove remained a relic of the past.

Fundraisers were held to help defray the costs of restoration to the Squirrel Cage Jail. At the time, the posters promoted it as the only rotary jail in the world. It was the only three-story jail of this design ever built.

A corner of the kitchen before restoration, the stove vent hole at the top of the wall.

By April of 1971 the Pottawattamie County Board of Park Commissions proposal for preservation of the jail was received in the hands of MAPA, the Metropolitan Area Planning Agency for a vote to decide the fate of the jail. The proposal estimated that the cost to preserve the building would be $21,000 with funds to be split 50/50 from federal money and local funds. In the meantime, steps were being taken to nominate the

Squirrel Cage Jail for inclusion on the National Historical Register by the Iowa State review committee for historic sites. Their estimated costs came to $16,000 and included landscaping and sidewalk.

July of 1972 saw the historic jail open to the public, offering tours in the afternoon from 1:00 to 5:00, Tuesday through Saturday, and Sunday from 2:00 to 5:00. The fee was $1.00 for adults and fifty cents for children. The Squirrel Cage Jail had recently been designated on the National Registry of Historic Places. The open house was a call to raise awareness of this unique structure and bring in some much-needed funds for restoration. One of the first things on the agenda was to remove the white paint on the exterior brickwork and display the original red brick. A desire to restore the revolving cell mechanism was also on the list of planned restorations. Interest in the old building was evident as nearly 500 people came to tour the jail.

The warden's office in the process of restoration.

Destructive waves of influence swept across the nation, threatening historical buildings with the lure of money made available to sweep the old out of the way and replace it all with something new. It was a mindset that was to lead to the destruction of downtown Council Bluffs, and many other older sections of cities across the nation. In 1973 the promise of federal funds in the form of grants to revive decaying downtown areas across the country caught the attention of people in Council Bluffs. This 'urban renewal' decimated the old downtown along Broadway. This same mentality to sweep away the old and build new threatened the Squirrel Cage Jail as well.

Finally, in the early 1970's, the Historical Society bought the Squirrel Cage Jail and preserved it as a museum. There are currently only three jails built in this style still standing in the country. The Council Bluffs Rotary Jail is the only three-story structure of its kind. In the summer of 1973 work was being done on the exterior of the jail.

The board and volunteers have worked diligently to repair the jail and create a unique experience for visitors. There are plans in the works to reengage the mechanism to allow the cage to once again turn as it did originally.

The laborious job of removing the layers of white paint from the bricks was undertaken, as well as a new roof and numerous exterior repairs moved at a slow but steady pace.

The jail as seen from the alley standing between the two courthouses. The struggle to preserve the jail was a battle fought over a ten-year period.

A MOST HAUNTED PLACE IN IOWA

As the sun begins to set, the last rays of the dying light stream in through the bars belying the grim interior and desolate atmosphere of a jail. Soft mists arise and time warps into another plane, for soon, as the shadows of night descend, the spirits of those long since dead will cluster once again about the cells, the recreational and work areas that they knew for a time. Voices whisper between the walls and through the vacant cells, to weave between the bars a tapestry of whispered sound remembering the past. Children laugh and play once again, their soft giggles heard in the stillness of the fourth floor; a forgotten prisoner scrapes his tin cup against the bars calling for attention as the warden ambles through the building making sure everything is as it should be.

Sunlight streams in the windows of the bullpen, through the area that was once a shower, and stretches across the chipped concrete floor. The misty air begins to stir awakening the spectral figures of those long gone.

Strange events occur in the stillness of the night as shadow-forms are seen only in the corner of someone's eye, if they happen to be there. Look away, something has shifted; look back quickly, and the silence and stillness hold the visitor like a powerful embrace of long-lost friends. The rotary device and cells are precisely where the last turn on the rotary device stopped in December of 1969 and it has not moved since, save for another world on the other side of the veil. Does that create a special portal in time that opens to the door of the spirit world?

Stories of spectral visions have been related about the jail from its earliest days. One source has related that the Squirrel Cage Jail was built upon the site that had been the morgue of St Paul's Episcopal Church.

Do the spirits of the dead wander the jail?

Warden Robert A. Heller, his wife, Eva Heller who was also the cook, and their daughter Margaret Heller pose at the main entry of the Pottawattamie County Jail in 1916. Some claim to hear the sounds of children at play in the fourth-floor apartments of the jailer.

So many structures such as jails carry the energies of desperation, anger, frustration and lost hope. All of these combine to create a place that could easily retain the spirits of some who have spent time in such a place. Who could these spirits be? Some of the investigators believe they have an idea who some of these restless spirits might be. All of them agree that there is plenty of activity in the Squirrel Cage jail.

Those who seek to unravel the mystery of a haunting often look to see who may have died in a certain place. There were only four deaths within the Squirrel Cage Jail.

The accidental shooting of Special Deputy Claude Dail occurred during the Farmer's Holiday Revolt in 1932. During a demonstration of a riot gun by Deputy Sheriff Kinsell the weapon accidently discharged a round, striking Dail, mortally wounding him. He was taken to the hospital and died two hours later.

Thomas Reifle hung himself in his cell on April 22, 1897. Reifel was awaiting grand jury action on charges of bootlegging. He was arrested on April 6 at his home in Red Oak by Deputy U S Marshall Eller and brought before the U S Commissioner George F. Wright of Council Bluffs. Defaulting in his bail he was placed in the county jail. A bond was prepared and sent to a number of his friends in Red Oak; however, they refused to sign. This made Reifel despondent that no one would sign the bond for him. He remained morose for several days, his melancholy mood caused him to pace endlessly up and down the corridor where he was housed on the second tier with other federal prisoners. On the afternoon of his death he had asked another prisoner if a man could successfully take his life in one of the cells. The question was forgotten until Reifle was discovered dead the next morning.

Reifle's dead body was discovered in the morning leaning against the wall by jailer Al Morgan, who was letting prisoners out of their cells and into the corridors before breakfast. Reifel's cell was number twenty on the second tier. He had tied a towel to the crossbar above the cell door and attached a linen cord, the end of which he wrapped about his neck.

He leaned forward, thus slowly strangling to death. Since there was not room for him to simply drop and be suspended from the cord, he had to opt for a slower, more painful method. The linen cord was no bigger than a fishing line and cut deeply into this neck. His swollen tongue protruded from his mouth. His death was slow and painful. The cord he used had been used by the prisoners as a clothes line in the common area. Before being locked up for the night he managed to take it down and hide it in his pocket. Other prisoners in nearby cells said they heard nothing in the night. Immediately upon discovery, Coroner Jennings was called in. He ruled it was clearly a case of suicide. The body was taken to Undertaker Estep's rooms for preparation for burial.

This had been Reifle's second stint in the jail. The previous year he was arrested by federal authorities for sending letters through the mail to a young woman in Red Oak that contained obscene language. For this charge he pled guilty and threw himself on the mercy of the court. Due to extenuating circumstances his case was suspended. It was after this he got into the bootlegging business acting as a book agent.

Reifle, age forty-nine, was a native of Germany but had lived in Iowa for the last twenty-three years. In the past he had been in more comfortable circumstances but fell on hard times. His wife had died previously, and he had two daughters. It was reported that he had a brother in Red Oak in the clothing business, who was successful and quite wealthy. Thomas Reifle is buried in Fairview Cemetery in Council Bluffs.

July 19, 1907. A prisoner, Harry Cohan, a junk dealer in Des Moines, age forty-four died of a heart attack. It was reported in the newspaper that Harry Cohan smoked between 150 to 200 'paper pipes' a day. He even bragged that he smoked 300 'coffin nails' in a twenty-four period. On the morning he died he got up and had begun to sweep out his cell, as was routine for the prisoners. Jailer Gallup noticed that Cohan looked unwell, even pale. He asked another prisoner to clean up Cohan's cell. As Cohan walked across the corridor to sit down and rest, he suddenly gasped for breath, and fell backwards. Another prisoner caught him as he fell, and there were attempts to resuscitate Cohan.

Two weeks earlier Cohan had been sentenced to thirty days for stealing brass and iron from the Rock Island train yards in Council Bluffs. While incarcerated he made no complaints of illness to the jailer. He did mention to a fellow prisoner that he did have a weak heart and had experienced some chest pains a week earlier. Maybe having an inkling of his impending death, he commented that he should make a will claiming to own $30,000 worth of property. He rarely spoke of his family but, shortly before he died, he talked about how he wanted to leave what he had to his son and daughter in Philadelphia.

A strange occurrence happened shortly before Cohan suffered his fatal heart attack. Another prisoner, Lafayette Daley, serving a sentence for shooting a young man in the west end, told others that he had seen a vision of a large man with a dark complexion fall dead in the corridor of the jail and his body carried out through the iron door of the first floor. The description certainly fitted Harry Cohan. Little was thought of Daley's talk at the time, but when Cohan died a number of prisoners recalled what Daley had said.

The coroner's finding was that Harry Cohan had died immediately upon falling. When Cohan's son, a keeper of a cigar store, was notified, he stated that he did not want the body. Harry Cohan was buried by the county.

May 23, 1942. The prisoner Joseph Letak, age forty-four, of 2239 North 19th Street in Omaha, fell to his death in the jail. The coroner's verdict at the inquest ruled that his death was due to his own negligence. Letak, a tailor, was being held in the jail on a charge of larceny and, according to other prisoners, had been moody in the last few days before his death. He was worried about the charge against him and being sentenced to the state penitentiary. Letak had managed to climb up to the third tier of cells to the catwalk, even though he and all other prisoners were regularly admonished to stay off of it. The catwalk is a 30-inch wide steel plate that runs half way around the case of the bullpen. It was installed for emergency use in order to get to a prisoner's cell without disturbing the other inmates. A two-inch high flange skirts the edge of the catwalk toward the center of the bullpen where the other side is fastened to the cage.

Jailer Bastin was taking prisoners up to the second level of cells when he heard an unusual amount of noise coming from the first floor. When he went to investigate, he was informed by some of the prisoners that Letak had climbed up to the third tier and had fallen off the catwalk some twenty-feet to the concrete floor below. Bastin notified the sheriff's office and a doctor. Letak was taken by police ambulance to the hospital. He did not survive the fall. Upon inspecting the body, the coroner, L. H. Tyler, ruled the cause of death was a severe skull fracture and body bruises all due to the fall.

John W. Nose, a prisoner who witnessed the fall, told authorities that Letak climbed up the cage to the third-floor catwalk, then climbed back down to the second-floor catwalk. When he looked again, Letak was back up on the third level sitting on the catwalk with his back against the cell. His feet were pulled up against the flange at the edge. Nose looked away again but heard Letak holler and looked up to see Letak was standing up: he fell outward, face forward. He seemed to fall sideways and landed on his head on the concrete floor, then rolled over on his stomach. Nose stated that, though they were told not to climb up to the catwalk, some men did it anyway because it was cooler up there.

Eugene Criswell of 705 South 12th Street was playing bridge in a corner of the bullpen and glanced up and saw Letak sitting on the third-floor catwalk. Two minutes later the man fell to the floor. Criswell recalled that Letak, the night before, had told him about his troubles at home and seemed very down the last few days before his death. The day before Letak had been in an argument with a few other inmates and some prisoners put a "lighted cigarette" in his pocket.

Another prisoner, Roy Baker said it was his job as judge of the kangaroo court, prison justice among inmates, to maintain order and had warned the others not to go up there. He added that Latek mentioned that he'd been feeling dizzy of late. He also commented that Letak had been moody, cheerful for a while, then depressed, then cheerful again and so on.

If the timing is just right, sometimes as the sun is setting, the intense light streams in the barred windows and a slight haze is seen to rise from the floor on the first level. Is it a play of light or the spirits of those long since released returning once again still tied to the jail?

Phantom figures walk the corridors, sheriff's deputies still go about their appointed rounds and prisoners inhabit their cells still serving sentences long since passed. Too often there are sounds that cannot be explained and, though the jail may be draughty, there are also numerous cold spots that cannot be explained. Some people upon entering the jail are immediately overtaken by a feeling that they are not alone. Women visitors often complain of a tugging at their hair. Some visitors have left a room only to return to find pictures have fallen off the wall.

The Squirrel Cage Jail has been designated one of the most haunted places in Iowa. Numerous paranormal investigative teams have dared to spend the night alone in the jail with whomever walks there from another dimension. None of the teams have departed without some unexplained experience happening to them. Voices murmur, cold spots persist, shadows are cast from forms no longer living, and lights move without explanation.

Apparitions have been seen by numerous groups investigating the jail for spectral inhabitants. A figure of a man in full uniform has been seen often. Also, a little girl in a gray dress. Women have been seen in the women's detention area. There are unexplained noises and often things will fly off the shelves when no one has touched them. There is a man who must be thirsty in his cell, for the sound of a tin cup clanking against the bars can be heard while no one is seen.

The volunteers and staff have had many experiences in the jail. Keys are heard to rattle on the forth floor, whispers and even a music box will play. Children will laugh and play hurrying about the apartment rooms. While working up there, in another room, a door can be heard to open and when checked the door is always tightly shut. The forth floor is said to be the most haunted.

A photograph of the white-washed jail, looking down from the old courthouse, invites visitors to take a step back in time and visit the Squirrel Cage Jail Museum. The old summer kitchen can be seen in this photograph.

For some time, the Squirrel Cage Jail has been offering ghost tours to people who have interest in such venues. Time after time the spirits that reside at the jail have never failed to manifest in some way. I know that when I was exploring the jail for the creation of this book, I had a number of experiences. First, on the 4th floor where the family lived, I heard the giggles of two little girls, and there was no one but myself and the director. As I sat in the office one day quite alone I sensed a man who looked around the door to see if I was friend or foe of the jail. He gave me a curt nod and a smile before moving on his rounds. He guards the jail from those who do not think well of the place.

Ben Ediger of BNZ "Dead Time" Paranormal out of Kansas City came to the jail to investigate on October 6, 2018. He and his team had a number of baffling experiences and got some images on camera that cannot be explained. More than one of the team experienced a large cold spot in the infirmary. The readings on the Mel-Meter dropped eight degrees when held in the area of the cold spot. Investigators heard the clear calling out of the name 'Mary' followed by an annoyed reply, all when no one still living was in the room.

The most telling evidence Ediger produced was caught on film. He was able to capture a strange figure in a photograph taken on the third floor, where those prisoners were housed whose good behavior had earned the privilege of being a trusty.

In the photograph taken during the paranormal investigation the shadow figure of someone is clearly visible standing at the barred window. There are no trees outside this window, and nothing else to cast such a shadow.

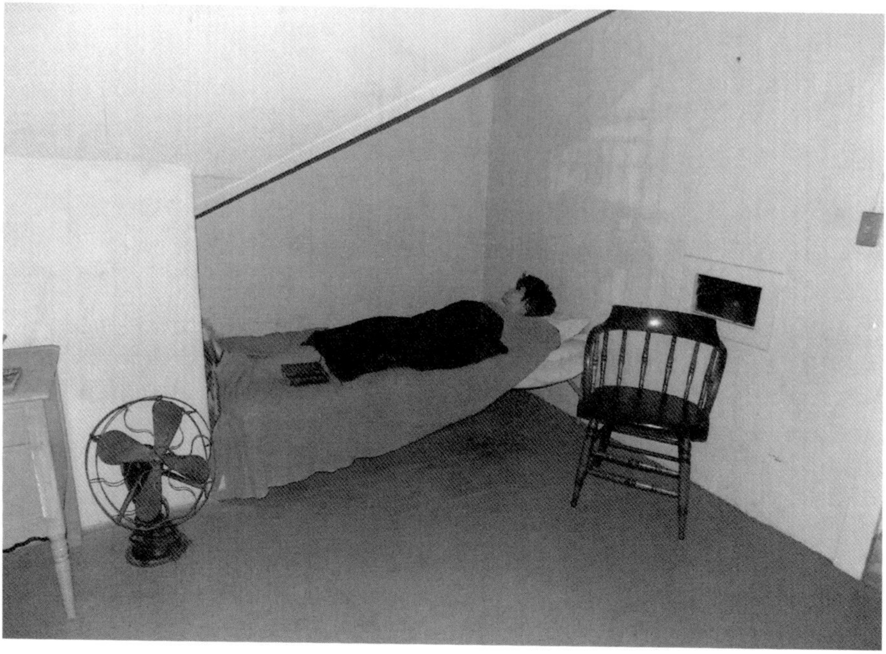

Ghost hunters, from Dead Time Paranormal, managed to take a curious photo in the trusties' room on the third floor. What appears to be the shadow of someone at the window could not be explained. There are no buildings or trees that could have cast the shadow.

An enlargement of the photograph from the trusties' cell displays a very male figure casting a shadow.

A strange photograph tells a great deal. Many people have taken a photo from that same angle, yet none has been able to duplicate the visage that appeared in Ediger's photo. A photograph taken by the author clearly reveals no shadow being cast.

An enlargement of the photo taken by Dead Time Paranormal shows a semi-transparent figure at the window. Is it just a play of the light or a spectral figure? Note how the head is semi-transparent and the bars are clearly visible, whereas the rest of the body is more substantial.

Another photograph taken of that same room has no such shadow.

In another investigation a sensitive walked onto the third level and said one word: Bird. At the time she had no knowledge of the most notorious prisoner ever housed in the Squirrel Cage Jail.

Jeremy Kurland and Christie Williams of Buried Alive Paranormal Productions were able to capture an image that they believe is the face of the jailer in the 1950's, and that of the last resident of the jail, Bill Foster in the fourth-floor apartment. As the two, and their team, moved about the jail, investigating, they reported that they heard footsteps, the shuffling of feet, and the sounds of children playing. They also noticed objects had moved.

In the women's detention area, a female investigator was seated on the iron bunk when she felt someone touch her. In the infirmary there was some unexplained energy that could be sensed at the place where an attempted jail break was patched over. In the residential quarters on the fourth floor, an image of someone in a warden's uniform was photographed at the window of the back room.

The EVP, an electronic voice phenomenon, is a device that many ghost hunters use to pick up noises that cannot be heard with the human ear. This is the wavelength where the voices of spirits can be heard. A voice is heard to say, "Otto." Also, giggles can be heard as well as a child's voice that says, "mom."

A man's face was seen by investigators on the fourth floor. A number of times photos seem to capture an image of a man in a brown uniform sometimes in the windowless room that is called the office, other times he is seen standing at one of the windows. Once when investigators were outside, someone looked up to see a figure of a man standing at the window looking down at them. Many believe this is Otto, a warden who never left.

Also, while investigators were busy on the third floor, the EVP on the fourth-floor, picked up the words: "Brokenness" and "Go!" This happened as one of the investigators got locked in a third-floor jail cell elsewhere in the building. They said that the sound of a child's laughter could also be heard on the first floor.

The Mel-Meter, another ghost hunting tool that measures the electromagnetic field as well as the temperature in a room, would go off and buzz as investigators moved about the jail. One place in particular where the Mel-Meter sensed a drastic drop in temperature was in the infirmary.

Another group came to the jail to investigate, and reported that they heard the voice of a little girl and the sound of laughter. Many in their group reported the feeling of being watched as they moved about the jail.

Some believe the presence of Jim M. Carter, who oversaw the construction of the jail and was said to be the first resident of the fourth-floor apartment, still lingers in the shadows. They claim that he has never left, and they could feel his presence during their investigation. Another possibility that investigators believe may be still there is Otto Gundath a former jailer.

Someone reported seeing a little girl dressed in gray playing in one of the cells, and shortly after felt a tugging at their clothing.

Evidently Bill Foster, who served from the 1950's to the close of the jail, refused to live in the fourth-floor apartment. He claimed that too much strange stuff happened up there. He complained of hearing footsteps, children's laughter and things being shuffled. He also noted that too often things were moved.

Some of the ghost hunters say that they saw a man's face at the window on the fourth floor when they were outside. Others have heard voices inside the jail, sometimes capturing them as an EVP on their equipment.

THE WALKING TOUR

The Squirrel Cage Jail, as it is referred to today, was originally known as the Pottawattamie County Jail serving as a jail from September 11, 1885 until December 1, 1969. Construction of the jail began in April of 1885 and took five months to complete. The cost to build the jail, according to an article in The Council Bluffs Globe, was about $30,000. Haugh & Ketchman's foundry in Indiana was paid $21,000 for the metal parts of the jail. It was cheaper to have them construct these pieces as this company had the specific sizes required, so that another foundry didn't have to create the unique metal parts. Whickham Brothers of Council Bluffs were the general contractors for the job. Many other Council Bluffs workers helped to construct the jail. John Epenter, G. S. Lawson and B. Terwillinger were some of the local Council Bluffs workmen engaged to help in the construction of the jail.

DESIGN

The design of the rotary jail was patented in 1881 by William Brown and Benjamin Haugh of Indianapolis, Indiana. The three-story Pottawattamie County Jail was the largest rotary jail constructed, of the eighteen jails of this design built across the Midwest in the 1880's. Only three of these unique rotary jails are still standing and all have been converted into museums. A single-story jail is located in Gallatin, Missouri and a two-story jail is located in Crawfordsville, Indiana. The three-story rotary jail is in Council Bluffs, Iowa.

DIMENSIONS

From the outside the design resembles more a carriage house of the era than a jail. Some interesting facts about the dimensions of the jail: the jail cylinder measures twenty-eight feet high and is twenty-four feet in diameter with a total weight of 90,000 pounds empty. There are ten cells per floor, a total of thirty cells in all. The jail cylinder is twenty-eight feet high and twenty-four feet in diameter.

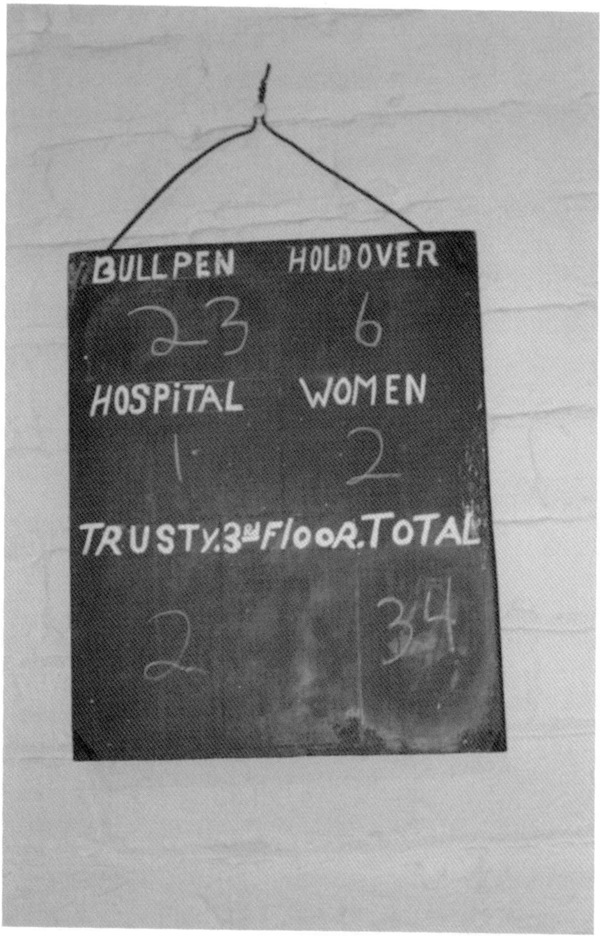

A chalkboard recorded the number of prisoners in the jail, and their locations. This hangs outside the warden's office.

SHERIFF'S OFFICE

Once a person was arrested, they were brought in through the double front doors and immediately into the sheriff's office. Upon entering the jail, iron stairs led up to the second level, a door on the right opened onto the sheriff's office and a doorway to the left opened onto the kitchen. Straight behind, under the stairs, was the entry to the first floor of the rotary jail, and the grub hole is visible, where food was slid through to the guard to feed the prisoners.

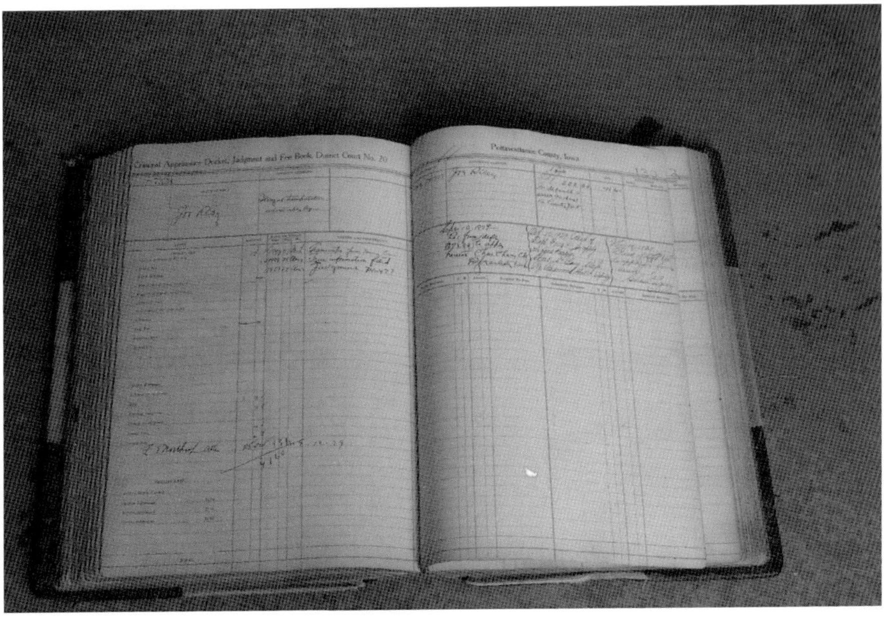

Old ledger books provide details of cases, reasons for incarceration and lengths of sentences.

Over the years the jail accumulated ledgers with detailed information pertaining to criminal dockets in municipal court in Council Bluffs, search warrant dockets for municipal court for the city of Council Bluffs, and criminal appearance and fee dockets for Pottawattamie County.

Transporting prisoners in manacles was employed to prevent trouble or escape. On display are various sets of handcuff devices used through the years.

Each inmate, after their arrest, would begin their time at the jail in the sheriff's office to be booked for their offense. This would be recorded in one of the large ledgers, entries written by hand: name, date, cause of commitment and duration of stay, including arrival and departure dates. Also recorded were details of the officer or judge who released them. As they were being booked, the jailer would take away any personal property of the inmate, as well as anything that could be considered dangerous such as shoelaces, belts, belt buckles, ties, and jewelry; however, a prisoner was allowed to retain cigarettes and matches. Items taken from any prisoner were also recorded in the ledger. Prisoners often had to be relieved of dangerous weapons. These are on exhibit in the hall outside the sheriff's office.

One of the first things the guards did when a prisoner was brought to the warden's office for processing, was to search each prisoner. On display are some of the sort of weapons taken from prisoners.

SOLITARY CONFINEMENT

Not all the prisoners brought into the jail were cooperative or on their best behavior. If any prisoner began to resist or misbehave in any way, they were placed in solitary confinement. This could happen if their actions at the time of their booking warranted time in solitary to cool down. If a prisoner made trouble from a cell or common area, they were also placed in the solitary confinement cell. The time the prisoners spent in solitary varied according to their conduct. Prisoners were usually placed in solitary for about thirty minutes to an hour. If they did not calm down and become cooperative they could be left in solitary until they were ready to behave. The longest time spent in solitary by any prisoner on record was ten days.

There are two doors to solitary. One entry is from the sheriff's office, with an iron plate door to dull the sounds of yelling if the prisoner continued to complain. The other is from the common area on the ground floor of the jail. The prisoners acting up at booking were placed into solitary from the office entry, while prisoners who misbehaved in their cells or common area were brought down the barred hallway into solitary. Either way, it was not a pleasant experience. The cell was extremely small and cramped, measuring six feet tall, and two feet by one foot wide. There was no way to sit down in this tightly confined cell. The inmate would be given bread and water twice a day and had only a coffee can or bucket to use as a toilet.

At times, if there was more than one prisoner to be kept in solitary confinement, the narrow hallway from the common area was utilized as a second cell. This was a little more comfortable than the regular solitary cell as this space allowed a man to lie down and stand up, a luxury not afforded the prisoner in the primary solitary confinement cell.

If a prisoner was uncooperative, they would be put into the solitary confinement cell to cool off. There are two doors to the solitary cell in the jail. This is the entrance from the warden's office. Solitary confinement is a narrow cell that allows the prisoner only room to stand. If the prisoner is in need of the bathroom, a bucket or old coffee can was left in the cell for this use. Most prisoners became compliant rather quickly after a short while in this cell.

There is also access to the solitary confinement cell from the bullpen on the first tier of cells. At times, if the solitary cell was already in use, the narrow hallway was utilized as a second solitary cell.

KITCHEN

Opposite the sheriff's office is the kitchen where all the meals were prepared. The meal preparation was the responsibility of the jailer's wife, also known as the jail matron. With a maximum capacity population of anywhere between sixty to ninety prisoners the preparation and serving of meals twice a day could be a daunting task. Trusties were enlisted to help serve the meals to the prison population.

In the early years of the jail, the kitchen stove was the only source of heat. The warden's wife would cook all the prisoner's meals and the trusties would help distribute the meals.

The coal burning stove in the kitchen is original to the building. It also served as the only source of heat for the building, as in 1885 central heating for the prisoners was not a consideration. Each day the matron would rise early and add coal to the banked embers of the fire from the day before. Coal burned in the stove was taken from the stove and distributed to heaters located around the building. It would be many years before steam heat using radiators would be added to the jail. The steam would be pumped from the boiler at the courthouse.

The door located on the southern wall of the kitchen was added in the 1920's, along with a summer kitchen. This summer kitchen would assist in cooking the quantity of food needed to feed the jail population and would ease the buildup of excessive heat in summer. Some of the graffiti on the walls of the cells relates the menus of the day. On alternating days, oatmeal or Cream of Wheat for breakfast. Dinner would vary from soup and chicken to noodles and wieners, with meat and potatoes on Sunday. For supper eggs, sandwiches, beans, potatoes and spaghetti were served.

On display in the kitchen are liquor bottles and beer cans from the late 1800's and early 1900's. They represent some the contraband smuggled in by prisoners that were found secreted away in the walls of the jail.

The lower shelf displays bottles and cans of liquor that were smuggled into the jail by trusties assigned certain tasks related to the needs of the jail. Many of these items were found hidden in holes and cracks in the walls when the building was being restored. These bottles date from the late 1800's to the early 1900's. The muffin tin belonged to Bridget Cody O'Neill who was jail matron from 1888-1892.

CELL BLOCK

Before entering the cell block there is a table with a model of the Squirrel Cage Jail. The three floors of the cells would rotate as a unit within the outer cage of bars. This rotation was powered by a hand crank at the opening of each floor. The mechanism was balanced in such a way that one man could easily turn the crank to rotate the cell blocks. This was achieved by interlocking gears.

A model of the jail gives visitors an overview of the jail complex and rotary device.

There was only one opening per floor into the cell block. This was to minimize the number of prisoners that would have access to the door. The jailer cranked the cylinder around to the desired cell when a prisoner would have some reason to be taken from his cell. The entry cab had a swinging door much like a cattle gate that allowed the jailer to direct the inmates one way or another for entering or leaving the cell block. Originally there were catwalks around the second and third floor levels, however these were removed many years ago.

It was in 1960 when everything changed for the jail as a penal institution. More and more the rotary cells were getting stuck. They were no longer able to scour, possibly due to the weight of the drum on the gear mechanism. As this was the only three-story rotary jail built, there are none to compare it to in terms of the failure of the inner workings of the gears. The jail continuously failed health inspections and was deemed as unfit for human habitation. Orders from the Fire Marshall demanded changes be made if the building was to continue serving as a jail. The jail ceased rotating in 1960 and holes were cut in the bars of the cells on the first floor, as well as for those cells where access by the platforms would allow. The fire escape was also changed at this time. Sanitation was spruced up and considered passable for use as a jail.

The jail would continue to serve for incarceration for another nine years before finally closing in 1969. In those final nine years the jailer refused to enter the cell block unless accompanied by an armed guard.

FIRST FLOOR CELLS

Like the prisoners imprisoned for their sentences, visitors must pass through the entry cab. On each side of the entry, behind the bars, are small shelves connected to a slit-like hole in the wall. This was known as the pass-through or grub-hole. Trays with food for the inmates passed through this slit and were given to the prisoners. Thus, the term grub-hole. Each floor has its own pass-through. The matron, her family and trusties would slide the food trays through the grub-hole. Another prisoner assisting inside the cell block would deliver the meal to the prisoner whose cell was rotated by the warden to the door to receive their meal. This consisted of a tray, cup, plate, spoon and the meal. Prisoners were not allowed knives or forks.

Just outside the kitchen is the grub hole. The trusties would deliver the food on trays to the other side of the wall where the rotary cells and bullpen were located. The jail makes use of the drop-down barrier, using it for the guest book.

Each cell is a pie-shaped room that would house two prisoners. The cells were furnished with two bunks, a bench and a toilet. The niche at the back of the cell was the toilet. Indoor plumbing was almost unheard of when the jail was built in 1885. The creators of the rotary jail created an ingenious method of flushing out the system with water and ventilation holes at the top of the recess allowed ventilation. There were issues with these toilets being jammed when prisoners would stuff them with the intention of blocking them, thus gaining a short respite from their cell while the toilet was unclogged. Access to the innerworkings of the plumbing was entered through the top floor in the ventilation shaft.

A prisoner would step through the secured doorway, past the opened rocker arm door and into a cell.

Depending on how a prisoner behaved they could be released into the common area. For those who did behave, they were allowed to congregate in the bull-pen area to read, talk, play cards and listen to the radio. One prisoner said that he would prefer a year in any other prison to a day in the confinement of the cells.

The section under the stairs in the common area is where the shower was located. It was dismantled years ago. The inmates showered using cold water while wearing their clothes. This also served as a rudimentary means of laundering their clothes. In the early years, the jail had no prison uniforms, and the men would wear whatever clothing they had on at the time of their arrest. In later years, laundry facilities were added utilizing the sort of washing machine on display in the shower area.

A vintage washing machine stands on display in what was the shower area for the first tier of prisoners. Before the installation of a washing machine prisoners would shower with their clothes on, as a means to also clean their clothes.

SECOND FLOOR

Those men who were housed on the second level of the jail had committed a more serious crime than the prisoners detained on the first floor. While the first-floor housed men on a short-term basis for crimes such as drunk and disorderly, theft and other smaller infractions, the men incarcerated on the second level could expect to be in the Squirrel Cage Jail from a month up to a year. Men housed here could also be awaiting trial or a transfer to another facility. Federal prisoners were also housed on the second tier of cells. This section has a much smaller day area, separated one on each side of the entrance door. This could be utilized by the jailer to keep men apart from one another.

Again, there are ten cells on this level; however, after 1960 when the rotary mechanism was dis-engaged, the jailer had only access to five of the cells. This meant less space to house the more dangerous criminals and added danger for the jailer. There is a small exercise room on either side of the entry to the second tier of cells. These would interconnect when the rocker arm of the cell block door was not engaged to transfer a prisoner. In case of emergency a hatch device would be able to be opened and prisoners could get to the main level bullpen.

On the second tier of cells is a common area that was used as a shower area instead of taking them down to the first floor. The cells would be rotated to allow one prisoner out at a time. By the entryway is the grub hole for the second tier.

When plumbing was added to the jail a shower area was installed in what had been a common area. The cell was rotated so the prisoner could exit and shower and then return to his cell. The cage would then be rotated by the warden to allow the next prisoner a shower.

There was an emergency door that could be opened in case of fire to allow the second tier of prisoners the means of escape to the first-floor level. Otherwise this was part of their common area and they could look down to the bullpen.

On display on the second-floor common area is the noose used in the last hanging in the State of Iowa.

On display is the noose used to take the life of Charles Noel Brown by hanging. He was the last prisoner executed in the State of Iowa at the Fort Madison State Penitentiary on July 24, 1962.

WOMEN'S DETENTION

The issue of housing women and juveniles called for separate quarters away from the men. The area over the sheriff's office housed the women and juveniles for their stay in prison. Women's crimes typically ranged from prostitution, gambling, and pick pocketing, to public intoxication, theft and forgery. At times, the women would have their children with them.

The women's cell block did not utilize a rotary device, instead, women's detention used conventional type of cells. There was a bathroom, shower and cells.

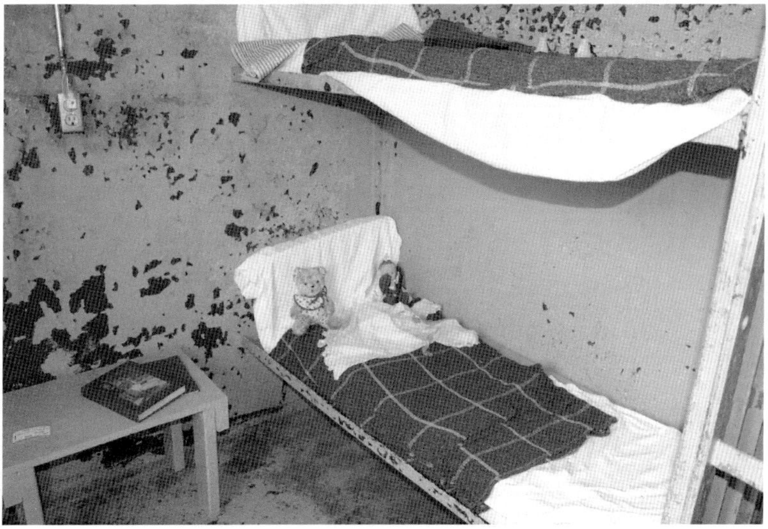

92. There were four beds to a cell, as many times the incarcerated woman had her children with her.

The women's shower was added once running water was added to the jail.

In the 1950's, because William Foster refused to live in the forth-floor apartment, a section of the women's detention was converted into his living quarters consisting of a bedroom, bathroom and a small closet.

The original cell door from what had been a unit of women's detention. Because Bill Foster refused to live on the fourth-floor, the area was converted for his personal use.

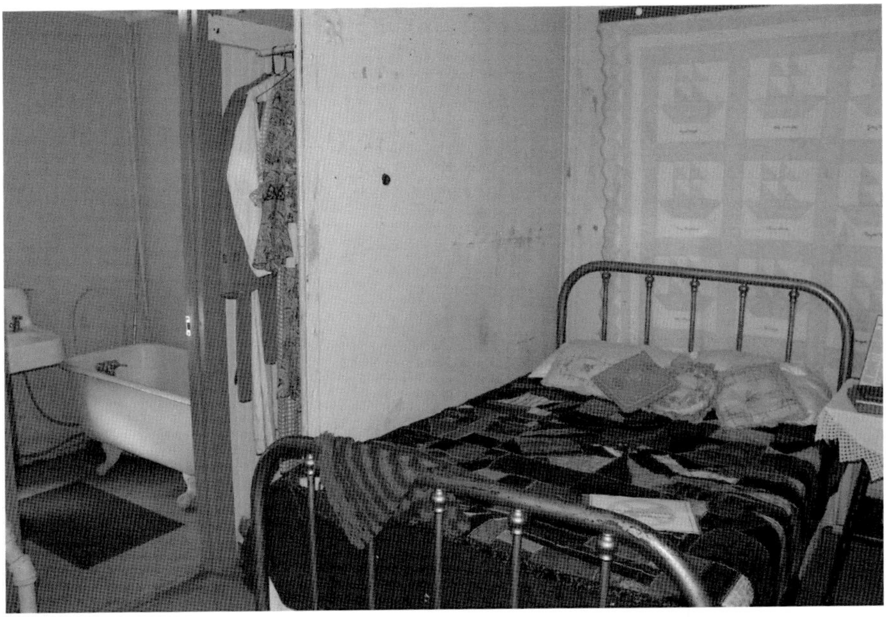

Warden Foster's quarters with a bedroom, bathroom and small closet.

THIRD FLOOR

The third floor of the jail housed the most dangerous criminals such as men charged with assault with a deadly weapon or murder. These were men like Jake Bird who went on a killing spree through the Midwest until he was finally caught and brought back to Iowa to await trial for his crimes.

The third tier of rotary cells housed the worst sort of criminals. Jake Bird was one such inmate. A mannequin is displayed in his cell. Some say his spirit still wanders the third level of the jail.

Outside of the rotary section of the jail, on the floor above the warden's rooms and the women's detention section, is the trusties' cell with a private bath and two beds. Across from it is the Infirmary.

After the jailbreak from the trusties' cell in the basement level, a section on the third floor in the front of the jail was converted to serve as the cell for the trusties. The trusties had a bed and a separate bathroom.

The door to the infirmary would be kept locked as any cell that held prisoners. A grub hole provided a delivery for the meals. The infirmary displays a number of antiquated medical tools.

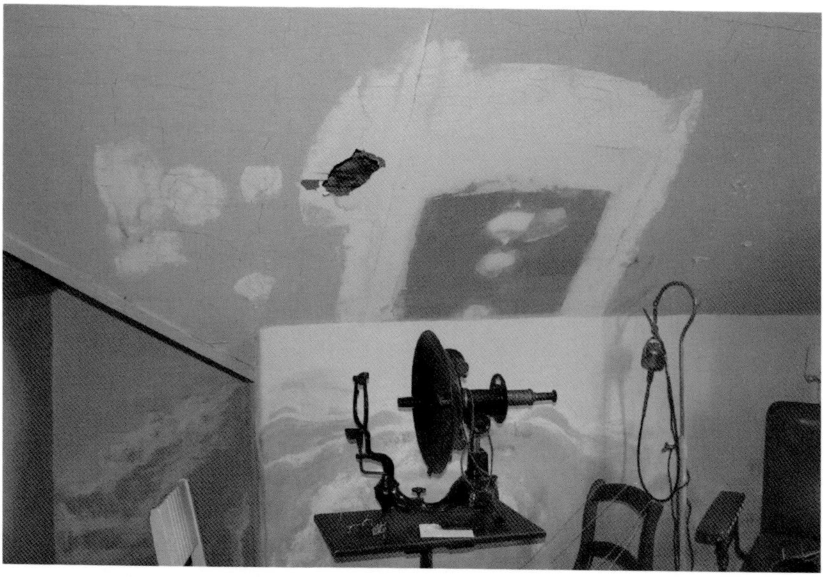

Prisoners in the infirmary also sought to break out of the jail. The eave wall shows patches where prisoners attempted to pound through the plaster and escape.

Looking out of the infirmary window on a frosty cold day. For many years there was no central heating in the building. The only room that generated any heat was the kitchen.

Throughout the prison system, the trusties were prisoners who had earned a degree of trust within the penal system and were allowed more freedom of movement than other prisoners. Their good behavior while incarcerated is how this designation of trusty was earned. These prisoners would assist the warden's wife in delivering the meals to the prisoners, and other various duties assigned. Trusties also performed various jobs around the jail as needed.

The infirmary is a single room where the doctor would tend to the prisoners. Many of the inmates would stick an arm or leg out between the bars as the guard turned the crank to rotate the prisoners in their cells. The results were broken limbs; according to local legend some had severed limbs, but there is no evidence in the records to support this. The wounded prisoner hoped for some time away from the cramped cage cell. They would be taken to the infirmary and patched up, usually within a few hours, and returned to their cell. General complaints of prisoners were attended to as needed by the doctor. It was rare for any prisoner to be housed for any length of time in the infirmary, but there was accommodation for just such circumstances.

At times prisoners sought to escape through the infirmary. The walls show patches where prisoners tried to punch out a wall or ceiling in hopes of escape. None of them ever succeeded.

There was a doctor on call for the jail.

leaving the third floor, climbing up the iron stairs to
the residential quarters of the warden.

FOURTH FLOOR

The Fourth floor was off limits to any of the inmates. The residential quarters are located directly above the rotary and bullpen areas of the jail. It was reserved solely to be used as the living quarters for the jailer and his family, consisting of eight rooms. Upon entering the residential apartment, visitors are in an entry area. On each side of this room are three windowless rooms, most likely used as storage or an office. A little further on are two rooms on opposite sides of the entry, to the right is a bedroom. In this room there is an area that was not utilized and is called the secret room. A hole was made in a section of the wall in order to see into this mystery area. It is unfinished and the bricks of the walls are evident when looking through the hole. One thing about this room is the strong draft that sucks air through it when the hole is uncovered. Opposite the bedroom, is the bathroom. At one time this had been another bedroom and was remodeled when plumbing was added to the building.

The private residence of the warden and his family. In the bedroom the wide windows let in plenty of light and were set up for cross ventilation in the summer.

In the bedroom, behind the wall, is what is considered a secret room. There is no explanation for why this space was not utilized. A hole was put in the wall to explore the space, and when it is left uncovered there is a strong updraft.

Originally there was no plumbing, even for the warden and family. However, when running water was installed, a room was converted into the bathroom.

Straight ahead in the entry area is the central core of the building that contains the maintenance hatch for the internal sanitation system for the cells. Opening the door that looks like it might be a closet, above is the copula and below are the ten hatches that mimic the pie-shape of the cells. An immense I-beam supports this internal section of the jail. A massive wrench sits atop the I-beam to be used to open the hatches and do maintenance work. Looking down through the grates glimpses of light can be seen that come through the toilet system. A prisoner twice made the attempt to escape by way of the sanitation core. He was, each time, captured and returned to his cell. Another feature about this core is that with the door open all the sounds from the cells below carry up the core and nearly everything can be heard. One can imagine that the fragrance on this floor would be most unpleasant in the heat and humidity of the summer.

Moving further into the apartment and around the core, the hallways encircle this core and behind it there is a family sitting room where the jailer would entertain friends with card games and other amusements. Each jailer and his wife would use the rooms as they desired.

A family area provided a place for the warden or his family to entertain, have friends over for a game of cards and good conversation that did not focus on the inmates below.

In an interview with a local woman of Danish descent, she related a story about her aunt who was married to one of the jailers in the early 1900's. She took one look at the accommodations and flatly refused to live in the jail.

Bill Foster, the last jailer to serve, refused to live in those rooms saying that too many strange things went on up there. He claimed that he heard footsteps, shuffling sounds and children's voices. He also noted that things would move on their own.

THE BASEMENT

The basement originally housed the support and gear mechanisms under the rotary section of the jail. A special cell for the trusties was located under the dining area of the jail, until a jail break made authorities question the placement of the cell. The iron bars at the windows were removed and left on the floor since they were too heavy to carry out of the jail. They are still there today.

Other staircases led to the basement under storm cellar doors. These entryways and all lower level windows have been sealed up and buried or concreted over. When a heating system was installed in the jail, the boiler was placed in the basement.

This level is not open to the public.

ABOUT THE AUTHOR

S. M. Senden was raised in Winnetka, a north shore suburb of Chicago. From an early age history, reading and writing were passions, as was travel. Senden has studied, lived and worked in the USA, Europe, the Mid-East and Africa, spending a number of years as an archaeological illustrator for various expeditions. S. M. Senden earned a Master's Degree and has studied creative writing, playwriting and screenwriting.

S. M. Senden has worked as a forensic artist with the police to identify murder victims in recreating the face from the skeletal remains.

Publications include: Murder mysteries: *Clara's Wish, Lethal Boundaries, Murder at the Johnson House,* and *A Death of Convenience and other Short Stories.* History books: *Red Oak* and *Montgomery County, Iowa* published by Arcadia in the Images of America series and *Lost Council Bluffs* published by the History Press. Short Stories: *The December Bride* in *Winter Wonders,* and *Christopher's Egg* and *Hog Wild and Pig Crazy* in anthologies. Articles and meditations in both *The Clergy Journal* and *The Word in Season,* ghost stories published in various magazines and a by-line in numerous newspapers.

Officer Bat Masterson was photographed with the latest equipment for the Pottawattamie County Sheriff's Department. The crime kit was transported to the scene of the crime.

BIBLIOGRAPHY

Babbitt, Charles H. Early Days at Council Bluffs Washington DC Press of Byron S. Adams 1916

The Palimpsest Volume XLII #9 September 1961

History of Pottawattamie County, Iowa. O. L. Baskin & Co,. Historical Publishers Lakeside Building Chicago, 1883

Craig, J. P. Messervey, R. A. McMillen, F. H Council Bluffs Iowa. Illustrated Des Moines, IA Miller & Watters, Letter Press and Binders. 1887

Field, Homer H and Reed, Hon. Joseph R. History of Pottawattamie County, Iowa from the earliest times to 1907. S. J. Clarke Publishing Chicago 1907

The City of Council Bluffs, Pottawattamie County, Iowa and the Trans-Mississippi and International Exposition Souvenir. Published by John C Small 1898

Miller, Lieutenant Robert L. A Selected History of the Council Bluffs Police 1853-2003 Printed by Copycat Inc. 2003

Petersen, Calvin J. The History of Fire in Council Bluffs.

Prassel, Frank Richard. The Western Peace Officer A legacy of Law and Order, University of Oklahoma University Press 1972

The Council Bluffs Nonpareil.